Berlitz®

Hong Kong

Front cover: Hong Kong by night

Right: lion dancers are a popular part of Hong Kong's festival calendar

TOP 10 ATTRACTIONS

Man Mo Temple • The air here is always heady with incense *(page 30)*

New Territories • Dramatic scenery, fringed with plenty of secluded beaches *(page 45)*

Glittering skyscrapers • Central district is home to an array of modern structures *(page 23)*

The Tiantan Buddha on Lantau • The world's tallest seated bronze statue of the Buddha *(page 53)*

Flagstaff House • Hong Kong's oldest colonial building now houses the Museum of Tea Ware *(page 26)*

Cheung Chau • Step down a gear on this small, laid-back outlying island *(page 55)*

Shopping • Day or night, an experience not to be missed *(page 77)*

The Star Ferry • The most exciting way to cross Victoria Harbour *(page 23)*

Man Fat Tze • The Monastery of 10,000 Buddhas *(page 49)*

Victoria Peak • A ride to the top on the famous Peak Tram provides some stunning views over the city *(page 27)*

CONTENTS

32

42

86

96

48
38

Features

INTRODUCTION

Exciting, mysterious, glamorous – these words have described Hong Kong for over a century. With its vibrant atmosphere and night-and-day activity, Hong Kong is an intoxicating place. There is no doubt that Hong Kong is crowded – it has one of the world's greatest population densities. But it is also efficient, with one of the best transportation systems anywhere, and, for such a crowded place, safe, with plenty of green peaceful places to escape to, away from the skyscrapers and traffic fumes. The shopping never ends – there's always another inviting spot just down the street. You'll find Hong Kong easy to get around, English spoken in tourist areas, and food that surpasses its reputation.

A New Era

On 1 July 1997 the British Crown Colony of Hong Kong reverted to Chinese sovereignty as a Special Administrative Region of the People's Republic of China. Today Hong Kong remains a capitalist enclave with its laws and rights intact, and China has promised that Hong Kong will continue in this fashion for at least 50 years. Beijing's declared policy of maintaining Hong Kong's prosperity and stability makes sense. Hong Kong has long been China's handiest window on the West, and the city is unrivalled in its commercial know-how and managerial expertise. Around the time of the transition there was much speculation about how things would change. But, in fact, once news of the handover vanished from the front pages, the people of Hong Kong returned to their usual topics of conversation: the economy and the price of housing.

There have been changes, of course, many of them due to economic progress, new construction and other factors that influence cities all over the world. And there's not a great deal of Britain left. Establishments are no longer preceded by the world 'Royal', Queen Elizabeth has vanished from the coinage, and the Union Jack has been replaced by the flag of China and the new Hong Kong flag with its bauhinia flower. You're far more likely to hear Mandarin on Hong Kong's streets than English now. It has become much easier for mainlanders to get travel permits to the SAR, and with the increasing affluence of many across the border there has been a surge in the number of Chinese tourists – 13.6 million visited in 2006, the biggest group by nationality. And in terms of expats, there are now more Americans working here than British.

People and Customs

With a population of seven million and a total area of just over 1,100 sq km (425 sq miles), housing is one of Hong Kong's perennial nightmares. To alleviate the problem, the government has become the city's major landlord with the construction of massive residential blocks. Though they have every modern facility, new flats average an internal floor area per person of only around 11 sq m (120 sq ft). Whole cities have been created in the New Territories, although the unimaginative architecture of these towns has been criticised.

Of Hong Kong's population, 95 percent are of Chinese descent. The majority are Cantonese, born in Hong Kong,

Fragrant Harbour

Hong Kong's name is derived from the Cantonese phrase for 'Fragrant Harbour' – *Heung Gong*. The evocative name probably derives from the trade in locally-grown incense wood, which once thrived in what is now Aberdeen. Another theory ascribes the name to the bauhinia, an aromatic flower which is native to the region and is now the logo of the Hong Kong administration.

or from South China, but there are immigrants from all over China. The Chinese people have been described as hardworking and pragmatic, attributes that have contributed immensely to Hong Kong's success. There are many stories of refugees who arrived with nothing in their pockets, set up a small pavement stall, worked diligently until they had their own shop, and then expanded it into a modest chain.

Morning group dancing in Victoria Park

Old customs are still followed: fate and luck are taken very seriously, and astrologers and fortune-tellers do a steady business. Before a skyscraper can be built, a *feng shui* investigation must take place to ensure that the site and the building will promote health, harmony, and prosperity. You'll also notice that gambling is a passion, whether it be cards, mahjong, the lottery, or the horses. Hong Kong has two major racecourses as well as an intensive off-course betting system for punters, and at the weekend the ferries to Macau are crowded with people on their way to the casinos.

What to See

Sightseeing in Hong Kong starts at sea level with the enthralling water traffic – a mix of freighters, ferries, tugs, junks and yachts. Views of the city and the harbour are panoramic. From the heights of Victoria Peak, or from skyscrapers and hotels, the views are especially exciting at night when the horizon comes alive in a blaze of lights.

The business and financial centre and the soaring architecture are on Hong Kong Island. Across Victoria Harbour, connected by the Star Ferry and MTR underground railway, is the Kowloon peninsula with its hotels, nightlife, and almost non-stop shopping. Beyond, in the New Territories, are a mixture of high-rise towns, the world's second-busiest container port, ancient walled villages, country parks and farms. Hong Kong's other, less developed islands, Lantau, Lamma and Cheung Chau, provide getaways. You can also take a ferry to Macau to find an entirely different kind of city, a rare blend of Chinese and Iberian culture.

It's anyone's guess what may happen in the future, but for now Hong Kong bristles with energy and ambition, and for the visitor, this beautiful city with its contrasts and variety is an exhilarating experience.

Despite the gleaming skyscrapers,
much of life in Hong Kong is played out at street level

A BRIEF HISTORY

In the popular mind, the history of Hong Kong, long the point of entry to China for Westerners, begins in 1841 with the British occupation of the territory. However, it would be wrong to dismiss the long history of the region itself. Archaeologists today are working to uncover Hong Kong's past, which stretches back thousands of years. You can get a glimpse into that past at Lei Cheng Uk Han Museum's 1,600-year-old burial vault on the mainland just north of Kowloon *(see page 44)*. In 1992, when construction of the airport on Chek Lap Kok began, a 2,000-year-old village, Pak Mong, was discovered, complete with artefacts that indicated a sophisticated rural society. An even older Stone Age site was discovered on Lamma Island in 1996.

While Hong Kong remained a relative backwater in the early days, nearby Guangzhou (Canton) was developing into a great trading city with connections in India and the Middle East. By AD900, the Hong Kong islands had become a lair for pirates preying on the shipping in the Pearl River Delta and causing a major headache for burgeoning Guangzhou; small bands of pirates were still operating into the early years of the 20th century.

In the meantime, the mainland area was being settled by incomers, the 'Five Great Clans': Tang, Hau, Pang, Liu and Man. First to arrive was the Tang clan, which established a number of walled villages in the New Territo-

Time travel

The *Hong Kong Story* at the Hong Kong Museum of History is the best way for a visitor to experience the territory's past. For just HK$10, you can travel from a point 400 million years ago to the 1997 handover. Exhibits are richly displayed and include replicas of an 18th-century fishing junk and a 1960s cinema.

Emperor Kangxi opened trade in Guangzhou on a limited basis

ries that still exist today. You can visit Kat Hing Wai and Lo Wai, villages with their walls still intact. Adjacent to Lo Wai is the Tang Chung Ling Ancestral Hall, built in the 16th century, and which is still the centre of clan activities to this day.

The first Europeans to arrive in the Pearl River Delta were the Portuguese, who settled in Macau in 1557 and for several centuries had a monopoly on trade between Asia, Europe and South America. As Macau developed into the greatest port in the East, it also became a base for Jesuit missionaries; it was later a haven for persecuted Japanese Christians. While Christianity was not a great success in China, it made local headway, as can be seen today in the numerous Catholic churches in Macau's historic centre.

The British Arrive

The British established their presence in the area after Emperor Kangxi of the Qing Dynasty opened trade on a limited basis in Guangzhou (Canton) at the end of the 17th century. Trading began smoothly enough, but soon became subject to increasing restrictions, and all foreigners were faced with the attitude expressed by Emperor Qianlong at Britain's first attempt to open direct trade with China in 1793: 'We possess all things,' said the emperor, 'I set no value on objects strange or ingenious, and have no use for your country's manufactures.'

Moreover, China would accept nothing but silver bullion in exchange for its goods, so Britain had to look for a more abundant commodity to square its accounts. Around the end of the 18th century the traders found a solution: opium was the wonder drug that would solve the problem. Grown in India, it was delivered to Canton, and while China outlawed the trade in 1799, local Cantonese officials were always willing to look the other way for 'squeeze money' (a term still used in Hong Kong).

In 1839 the emperor appointed the incorruptible Commissioner Lin Tse-hsu to stamp out the smuggling of 'foreign mud'. Lin's crackdown was indeed severe. He demanded that the British merchants in Canton surrender their opium stores, and to back up his ultimatum he laid siege to the traders, who, after six tense weeks, surrendered over 20,000 chests of opium. To Queen Victoria, Lin addressed a famous letter, pointing out the harm the 'poisonous drug' did to China, and asking for an end to the opium trade; his arguments are unanswerable, but the lofty though heartfelt tone of the letter shows how unprepared the Chinese were to negotiate with the West in realistic terms.

The Opium Wars

A year later, in June 1840, came the British retaliation, beginning the first of the so-called Opium Wars. After a few skirmishes and much negotiation, a peace agreement was reached. Under the Convention of Chuenpi, Britain was given the island of Hong Kong (where it had

An amusing isle

'Albert is so amused,' wrote Queen Victoria, 'at my having got the island of Hong Kong.' Her foreign secretary, Lord Palmerston, was not so amused; he dismissed Hong Kong as 'a barren island with hardly a house upon it.'

Causeway Bay in the mid-1800s

been anchoring its ships for decades), and on 26 January 1841, Hong Kong was proclaimed a British colony.

The peace plan achieved at Chuenpi was short-lived. Both Peking and London repudiated the agreement, and fighting resumed. This time the British forces, less than 3,000 strong but in possession of superior weapons and tactics, outfought the Chinese. Shanghai fell and Nangking was threatened. In the Treaty of Nanking (1842) China was compelled to open five of its ports to foreign economic and political penetration, and even to compensate the opium smugglers for their losses. Hong Kong's status as a British colony and a free port was confirmed.

In the aftermath of the Opium Wars, trade in 'foreign mud' was resumed at a level even higher than before, although it ceased in 1907. Opium-smoking continued openly in Hong Kong until 1946; in mainland China the Communist government abolished it in 1949.

Commerce and Wealth

The first governor of Hong Kong, Sir Henry Pottinger, predicted it would become 'a vast emporium of commerce and wealth'. Under his direction, Hong Kong began its march towards prosperity. It was soon flourishing; with its natural harbour that attracted ships, Hong Kong leaped to the forefront as a base for trade. Both the population and the economy began to grow steadily. A surprise was the sizable number of Chinese who chose to move to the colony.

In the meantime, the opening of Hong Kong was the last blow to Macau's prosperity. Inroads had already been made by the arrival of the Dutch and Macau's loss to them of the

Trading Houses

The Hong Kong of today owes its origins to the big trading houses or *hongs* of the 19th century. It was their top bosses or *taipans* who pressured the British government to secure a base to freely trade their opium and, once acquired, they were the driving force behind shaping the 'barren rock' into a successful trading port. Even today, places in Hong Kong bear the names of these big *taipans* as testament to their early power.

Rival *hongs* such as the Scottish Jardine, Matheson and England's Dent and Company were constantly squabbling among themselves. They were also at loggerheads with the government which was chasing taxes and urging better treatment of the local Chinese. To avoid paying taxes many *taipans* became honoury consuls of foreign powers or sailed their ships under foreign flags.

Many of these *hongs* still exist today, successful because they diversified as Hong Kong's economy changed. Their offices are now hidden in the morass of skyscrapers, their interests spread widely through subsidiaries, and some bought out by Chinese *taipans*. Although they no longer rule the roost, they still wield power from behind the scenes.

profitable Japanese trade. From then on, until its 1970s comeback with electronic and other export goods, Macau sank into relative obscurity.

Despite the differences between the Chinese majority and the European minority, relations were generally cordial. Sir John Francis Davis, an early governor, disgusted with the squabbling of the English residents, declared: 'It is a much easier task to govern the 20,000 Chinese inhabitants of the colony than the few hundreds of English.'

There were a few incidents: On 15 January 1857, somebody added an extra ingredient to the dough at the colony's main bakery – arsenic. While the Chinese continued to enjoy their daily rice, the British, eating their daily bread, were dropping like flies. At the height of the panic, thousands of Chinese were deported from Hong Kong. No one ever discovered the identity or the motive of the culprits.

Conditions in the colony in the 19th century, however, did not favour the Chinese population. The British lived along the waterfront in Victoria (now Central) and on the cooler slopes of Victoria Peak. The Chinese were barred from these areas, and from any European neighbourhood. They settled in what is now known as the Western District. It was not uncommon for several families and their animals to share one room in crowded shantytowns. So it is not surprising that when bubonic plague struck in 1894, it took nearly 30 years to fully eradicate it. Today in the Western District, you can still wander narrow streets lined with small traditional shops selling ginseng, medicinal herbs, incense, tea and funeral objects.

In 1860, a treaty gave Britain a permanent beach-head on the Chinese mainland – the Kowloon peninsula, directly across Victoria harbour. In 1898, under the Convention of Peking, China leased the New Territories and 235 more islands to Britain for what then seemed an eternity – 99 years.

The 20th Century

The colony's population has always fluctuated according to events beyond its borders. In 1911, when the Chinese revolution overthrew the Manchus, refugees flocked to the safety of Hong Kong. Many arrived with nothing but the shirts on their backs, but they brought their philosophy of working hard and seizing opportunity. Hundreds of thousands more arrived in the 1930s when Japan invaded China. By the eve of World War II, the population was more than one and a half million.

Old and new: the Old Supreme Court and Two IFC

A few hours after Japan's attack on the American fleet at Pearl Harbour in December 1941, a dozen Japanese battalions began an assault on Hong Kong; Hong Kong's minimal air force was destroyed on the airfield at Kai Tak within five minutes. Abandoning the New Territories and Kowloon, the defenders retreated to Hong Kong island, hoping for relief which never came. They finally surrendered on Christmas Day in 1941. Survivors recall three and a half years of hunger and hardship under the occupation forces, who deported many Hong Kong Chinese to the mainland.

A number of Hong Kong's monuments were damaged during this time: St John's Cathedral was turned into a military club, the old governor's lodge on the Peak was burned down, and the commandant of the occupation forces rebuilt the colonial governor's mansion in Japanese style.

At the end of World War II, Hong Kong's population was down to half a million, there was no industry, no fishing fleet, and few houses and public services.

Hong Kong Makes a Comeback

China's civil war sent distressing echoes to Hong Kong. While the Chinese Communist armies drove towards the south, the flow of refugees into Hong Kong gathered force, and by the time the People's Republic of China was proclaimed in 1949, the total population of Hong Kong had grown to more than two million people. The fall of Shanghai in 1949 brought another flood of refugees, among them many wealthy people and skilled artisans, including the Shanghai industrialists who became the founders of Hong Kong's now famous textile indus-

Housing for the masses

try. Housing was now in desperately short supply. The problem became an outright disaster on Christmas Day in 1953. An uncontrollable fire devoured a whole city of squatters' shacks in Kowloon; 50,000 refugees were deprived of shelter.

The calamity spurred the government to launch an emergency programme of public-housing construction; spartan new blocks of flats put cheap and fireproof roofs over hundreds of thousands of heads. But this new housing was grimly overcrowded, and even a frenzy of construction couldn't keep pace with the increasing demand for living space. In 1962 the colonial authorities closed the border with China, but even this did not altogether stem the flow of refugees: the next arrivals were the Vietnamese boat people.

Hong Kong's economy boomed in the 1970s and 1980s, thanks largely to its role as China's trading partner, and as a result the standard of living in the colony rapidly improved.

Back to China

As 1997 drew nearer, it became clear that the Chinese government had no intention of renewing the 99-year lease on the New Territories. Negotiations began, and in 1984, then British Prime Minister Margaret Thatcher signed the Sino-British Joint Declaration, in which Britain confirmed the transfer of the New Territories and all of Hong Kong to China in 1997. For its part, China declared Hong Kong a 'Special Administrative Region' and guaranteed its civil and social system for at least 50 years after 1997.

Although China's Basic Law promised that Hong Kong's existing laws and civil liberties would be upheld, refugees began flowing the other way. The British Nationality Act (1981) had in effect prevented Hong Kong citizens from acquiring British citizenship, and thousands of people, anxious about their future under China's rule, were prompted to apply for citizenship elsewhere, notably in Canada and Australia.

The protests in 1989 in Beijing's Tiananmen Square further increased tension with China. Some companies moved their headquarters out of Hong Kong.

Ironically, as the handover approached, the British granted the Hong Kong Chinese more political autonomy than they had done since the colony was founded, including such democratic reforms as elections to the Legislative Council.

Fresh Challenges

The transfer of sovereignty occurred smoothly on 1 July 1997, but the Asian economic downturn hit Hong Kong hard in the years that followed. Then, in 2003, Severe Acute Respiratory Syndrome (SARS) killed 299 people in the city, but its people showed great resilience. In July 2003 more than half a million protestors marched peacefully to protest against proposed anti-subversion laws. The following year 200,000 marched and established the tradition of annual 'July 1st marches', calling for more democracy and voting reforms. Early in 2005, Chief Executive Tung Chee-hwa resigned and was replaced by veteran civil servant Donald Tsang, popularly known as 'bowtie'. In March 2007, backed by Beijing, Tsang stood for re-election in Hong Kong's first-ever contested election for leader, against pro-democracy politician Alan Leong. The 'small circle' system, where just 800 people vote, guaranteed Tsang's re-election for a second term and Tsang led celebrations of the 10th anniversary of the establishment of the HKSAR in July 2007.

Hong Kong's destiny has always been linked to the water

Historical Landmarks

7th–9th centuries AD Probable arrival of the Tanka People. Chinese fortress constructed in Tuen Mun.

10th–14th centuries Arrival of the 'Five Great Clans' in what is now the New Territories.

1557 Portugal establishes official trading colony at Macau.

1699 British East India Company establishes itself in Canton.

1840 First Opium War sparked by a Chinese imposed ban on the opium trade operated by British and American traders.

1841 British fleet attacks Canton and takes possession of Hong Kong.

1842 Under the Treaty of Nanking, China cedes Hong Kong to the British 'in perpetuity'.

1856–60 The British embark on the Second Opium War and force the opening of further ports and the cession of the Kowloon Peninsula.

1898 Britain negotiates a 99-year lease of the New Territories and the 233 Outlying Islands, until 30 June 1997.

1911 Qing dynasty falls; Sun Yat-sen forms the Republic of China.

1935 Mao Zedong takes control of the Chinese Communist Party.

1941 Hong Kong surrenders to the invading Japanese.

1945 Hong Kong returns to being a British colony.

1950–53 Communist victory on mainland China sees massive waves of refugees swell the local population. Industrialisation commences.

1966–69 Cultural Revolution brings unrest to Hong Kong, but the colony remains intact as China's secret trade outlet.

1978 Reforms after the death of Mao Zedong foster increased economic links with China.

1984 Britain signs Joint Declaration for the return of Hong Kong to China.

1997 China resumes sovereignty of Hong Kong.

2003 SARS spreads in Hong Kong, killing 299 people.

2004 Beijing rules out universal suffrage by 2007.

2005 Tung Chee-hwa resigns. Donald Tsang becomes Chief Executive.

2007 HKSAR celebrates its 10th anniversary.

2008 Hong Kong hosts equestrian events for the Beijing 2008 Olympics.

WHERE TO GO

The crowded Kowloon peninsula and the booming New Territories on the mainland call for some serious sight-seeing; but we begin across Victoria Harbour on Hong Kong Island, where the city was first founded and which remains the centre of government, business and commerce.

HONG KONG ISLAND

Central District

No matter how many tunnels and transit systems speed up cross-harbour traffic, nothing matches the ride on the **Star Ferry** from Kowloon to **Central District** on Hong Kong Island across Victoria Harbour. As the green-and-white double-decker boats get ready to leave the pier, bells ring, the gangplank is raised and deckhands man the hawsers. On the 7-minute crossing the ferry weaves its way through an obstacle course of large and small craft, and the soaring skyline of Hong Kong Island draws nearer.

Thanks to land reclamation, the Star Ferry piers are closer together than ever. In late 2006, a brand new Edwardian-style ferry pier opened in Central District, situated on reclaimed land close to the Airport Express Hong Kong Station and the **International Finance Cen-**

A Star Ferry crossing the harbour in front of Two IFC

A galaxy of stars

There are 12 boats in the Star Ferry fleet, all with different star names: Morning Star, Northern Star, Golden Star, Meridian Star, Day Star, Solar Star, Night Star, Twinkling Star, World Star, Shining Star, Silver Star and Celestial Star. The oldest – Celestial Star – was built in 1956. Which one did you take?

tre (IFC). The IFC includes the Four Seasons Hotel, the IFC Mall and Hong Kong's tallest building, **Two IFC**. At 420m (1,378ft), Two IFC is the seventh tallest building in the world. Unfortunately, it has no viewing platform.

Walkways and footbridges connect all the main buildings in Central. From the IFC, footbridges across Connaught Road and Queen's Road Central lead to one of Hong Kong's curiosities, the 800-m (2,625-ft) long outdoor **Central Mid-Levels Escalator**. From 6am to 10am it ferries commuters

Feng Shui: Seeking Prosperity

Feng shui (or *fung shui* in Cantonese) literally means 'wind and water'. An ancient system of divination, its purpose is to achieve harmony with the forces of nature and produce an environment conducive to health and prosperity. Arranging physical premises according to the principles of *feng shui* deflects evil forces and assures the welfare of the inhabitants. Anyone moving into a new apartment will call in a *feng shui* geomancer to determine the optimum position of walls, doors and even furniture.

Buildings should face quiet water if possible, or have water nearby, such as a fish tank or a fountain. Lions and dragons are protective. The Hong Kong Bank's doors are guarded by a pair of bronze lions, and the China Resources Building by its Nine Dragons Wall. The famous Bank of China Tower, on the other hand, ignored *feng shui* principles, and is considered an untamed 'dragon's den'.

The dragons of Hong Kong must also receive consideration. New buildings must not block their accustomed pathways to the water, and in one case a new apartment block was constructed with a huge opening in its middle to allow the dragon's passage to the sea.

The Hong Kong Chinese are firmly committed to *feng shui*, and its principles are becoming popular in Europe and America. Inside China, however, visitors will find that such traditions are played down, perhaps in deference to what is considered a more 'modern' attitude.

from the Mid-Levels apartment complexes downhill to Central, then it runs uphill from 10.20am to midnight, giving a bird's eye view of street life in Central. The escalator travels above Cochrane Street to Hollywood Road, where a colourful 140-year old street market runs along Gage Street and Graham Street. Continue up the escalator past Hollywood Road and you'll arrive in **SoHo** with its cosy bars, trendy restaurants and quirky boutiques.

Modern design and bad *feng shui*: the Bank of China Tower

From the IFC you can also visit **Exchange Square**, home to the Hong Kong Stock Exchange, and continue east along the walkway to the **General Post Office**, which always has philately displays. Across the road is 52-storey **Jardine House**, with its porthole-shaped windows, and to the left is an underground walkway that takes you to **Statue Square**. On the east side of the square is one of the few colonial buildings left in the business district, the Legco Building (1912), which houses Hong Kong's governing body, the Legislative Council.

From Statue Square and nearby **Chater Garden**, look skywards to take in some contrasting modern architectural landmarks. Most famous is the striking 70-storey I.M. Pei-designed **Bank of China Tower**, not beloved by the people of Hong Kong – its triangular prisms and sharp angles violate the principles of *feng shui (see opposite)* and its radio masts stick up like an insect's antennae. The rival **HSBC Hong Kong headquarters building** is by Norman Foster; built on a 'coathanger frame', its floors hang rather than ascend. From inside the vast atrium you can view the whole structure as well as the mechanical workings of the building. Two bronze lions, carrying out *feng shui* principles, guard its doors.

You can catch one of Hong Kong's historic **trams** along Des Voeux Road and ride from Central to Causeway Bay *(see box, page 33)*. In 1904, the narrow, double-decker trams ran along the waterfront, but land reclamation has placed them far inland.

From the HSBC headquarters, cross Queen's Road Central and head up Battery Path to the 1917 French Mission Building, now used as the Court Of Final Appeal. Next door is **St John's Cathedral**. Built in 1847–49, this Anglican foundation is Hong Kong's oldest church and is thought to be the oldest Anglican church in East Asia. A mixture of neo-Gothic and Norman styles, the church was turned into a club for Japanese officers during World War II ; it was restored after the war. Note the stained glass windows in the Quiet Chapel, designed by Joseph Edward Nuttgens in the late 1950s.

Continue past the cathedral, take the footbridge across Garden Road towards Citibank Plaza and follow the signs for **Hong Kong Park**. The park's 10.5 hectares (25 acres) of landscaped gardens and lakes contains a large **greenhouse** that holds many species of plants, and an **aviary** of exotic birds.

In the park is **Flagstaff House**, Hong Kong's oldest colonial building, dating back to 1846. The two-storey whitewashed house now houses the **Museum of**

Inside St John's Cathedral

Flagstaff House, home to the Museum of Tea Ware

Tea Ware (open Wed–Mon 10am–5pm; free), with exhibits describing the history of tea from the Warring States period (475–221BC) to the present. Adjacent to the park is one of Hong Kong's largest and most up-market shopping malls, **Pacific Place**. Inside, it is packed with department stores, food halls, restaurants, art galleries, antiques shops and fashion boutiques.

Victoria Peak

For more than a century, the most exhilarating way up **Victoria Peak** (552m/1,713ft) has been by funicular. The **Peak Tram** (runs daily 7am–7pm) starts its scenic climb just across the street and around the corner from the American Consulate in Garden Road and makes its way, sometimes at a startlingly steep incline, to the upper terminus at 398m (1,305ft). The right-of-way travels past fancy apartment blocks, bamboo stands and jungle flowers. Passengers crane

The spectacular view of the city from Victoria Peak

their necks for dizzying glimpses of the harbour. The Peak is still the most fashionable place to live in Hong Kong, reflected in the astronomical property prices and rents. The Peak Tram, originally steam-powered, was built to speed the wealthy *taipans* to their mountainside retreats. Before the tram was built, sedan chairs and rickshaws were the only way to get here. Since the tram's inauguration in 1888 it has stopped only for typhoons and World War II.

The modern 120-passenger cars make the journey in around eight minutes. However, on sunny Saturdays and Sundays you may have to brave a crowd queuing up at the lower terminal. During the spring and autumn festivals, when people traditionally seek out the hilltops, the throngs are so large you would be better advised to try another time.

The upper terminus opens into the lower levels of **The Peak Tower** (open 10am–10pm; <www.thepeak.com.hk>), a distinctive wok-shaped building, packed with shops and plenty of dining options. Entertainment includes interactive games at the EA Experience on level one, a Madame Tussauds wax museum at podium one and the magnificent viewing terrace, which offers a 360-degree panorama of Hong Kong.

You can follow the **Peak Circle Walk** along Lugard and Harlech roads for impressive views of Hong Kong, the coastline and the islands in 45 minutes. The view is especially stunning at night. There are also souvenir stands, benches for a rest and some of Hong Kong's last surviving rickshaws – however these are not for rides, but are a tourist photo opportunity. If you're up to a climb, take the **Governor's Walk**, which winds up to the attractive **Victoria Peak Gardens**. These gardens used to belong to the governor's mountain lodge, but the building was demolished by the Japanese during the occupation of Hong Kong.

From the lower terminal of the Peak Tram, it's a short stroll along Upper Albert Road to **Government House**, which was home to 25 of the 28 colonial governors, and is now the official residence of the Chief Executive of the HKSAR, Donald Tsang. Across from the mansion, the **Zoological and Botanical Gardens** (gardens open daily 6am–10pm; zoo 6am–7pm; free) provide a welcome oasis. In the early morning the park is taken over by people doing *t'ai-chi* exercises. Both young and old perform ballet-like movements in slow motion to discipline the mind and body. The zoo has an interesting collection of jungle birds.

The Peak Tram

Western District

The Western District is one of Hong Kong's oldest neighbourhoods and its narrow streets hold a collection of fascinating traditional shops and enterprises. Opposite the Macau Ferry Terminal you'll find the **Western Market**, home to gift shops, cafes, fabric stalls and a unique Cantonese restaurant that hosts ballroom dancing every afternoon; it's situated in a four-storey Edwardian building built in 1906. For an interesting glimpse of small and family-owned shops, walk along Bonham Strand East and West, Man Wa Lane and Cleverly Street. You'll find herb and medicine shops, incense shops, chop makers' shops (makers of Chinese seals) and more.

It's also worth taking a walk along **Hollywood Road**, known for its antiques and curio shopping. The windows and open doors of the shops here reveal an alluring selection of Asian furniture, carpets, carvings, porcelain and bronze.

Also on Hollywood Road is the **Man Mo Temple** (open 8am–6pm), one of the island's oldest temples, dating back to the 1840s. Visitors entering the temple are confronted by a dense pall of smoke from all the burning joss sticks and the incense coils hanging from the ceiling (these will burn for as long as a month). The gold-plated sedan chairs on the left-hand side of the temple were once used for transporting the statues of the temple's gods in religious processions. The statues in the main shrine represent Man, the god of literature, and Mo, the god of war, a curious juxtaposition. The temple is always crowded with worshippers.

Chop maker at work

Just past the temple is the aptly named Ladder Street. Go down one flight of steps to Upper Lascar Row, popularly known as **Cat Street**, for more antiques and curio shops. The nickname apparently refers to the cat burglars who once sold their stolen goods here.

Walk up the steps to reach Caine Lane, where you'll find the **Museum of Medical Sciences** (open Tues–Sat 10am–5pm, Sun 1–5pm; admission fee). The interesting Edwardian building was formerly the Pathological Institute, founded to combat the 19th century's 30-year-long outbreak of bubonic plague. The old laboratory is still intact and there are also various interesting exhibits on the historical development of medical sciences in Hong Kong and on the interface between Chinese and Western medicine.

Wishes hang inside incense coils in the Man Mo Temple

Hong Kong University's campus is spread along Bonham Road. When it opened in 1912, the university had a total of 72 students; now it has around 14,000. At the top of a sloping driveway is the original Edwardian university building, now presiding over the institution's more recent structures. The University's **Fung Ping Shan Museum** (94 Bonham Road; open Mon–Sat 9.30am–6pm, Sun 1.30–5.30pm; free) holds a significant collection of antiquities: bronzes dating from 3000BC and ceramics that include Han Dynasty

Trams trundling along
Des Voeux Road

tomb pottery. It also has the world's largest collection of Nestorian crosses from the Yuan Dynasty period.

Wan Chai

Situated just to the east of the financial district, Wan Chai was once an area of sleazy clubs and topless bars; this was the setting for *The World of Suzie Wong*. Servicemen relaxing from the rigours of the Vietnam War poured millions of dollars into the Wan Chai boom of the 1960s. There's still a rash of tacky girly clubs here, but also plenty of regular pubs and a smattering of smart cocktail and theme bars.

The Wan Chai waterfront is dominated by the **Hong Kong Convention and Exhibition Centre** (HKCEC), which includes a huge exhibition space and two theatres. It hosted the 1997 handover ceremony. Just outside on the Wan Chai promenade the giant **Golden Bauhinia** statue commemorates the establishment of the HKSAR on 1 July 1997 – a must-visit for every mainland tour group. On the other side of Gloucester Road is the **Hong Kong Arts Centre**, with galleries, theatres and an arts cinema, and the **Hong Kong Academy for Performing Arts**, a popular venue for visiting international stage shows.

On Wan Chai's Bowen Road, **Maiden's Rock**, also called Lover's Rock, is the gathering place for the annual Maiden's festival. The rock is steeped in tradition. Every August young women convene to light joss sticks and some even climb the 9-m (30-ft) rock to pray for good husbands.

Causeway Bay and Beyond

About 2km (1 mile) east of Wan Chai, **Causeway Bay** is second only to Tsim Sha Tsui as Hong Kong's place to shop. A prosperous tourist district, it is full of shopping centres and department stores, along with a number of good restaurants. The busy night-and-day crowds make this area vibrant and lively.

On the nautical side is the **Causeway Bay Typhoon Shelter**, where expensive yachts are moored, and the Hong Kong Yacht Club has its headquarters. Across Gloucester Road, opposite the World Trade Centre, is the **Noon Day Gun**, which under British rule was sounded on the stroke of midday. Silent for a time, the tradition has been revived and is a tourist attraction.

It's not clear how the custom started. One story has it that traders Jardine, Matheson & Co fired a private salute for a

Take a Tram

The ancient tram system that travels along Des Voeux, Hennessy and Causeway roads is the most leisurely and revealing way to see Hong Kong. With more than 32km (20 miles) of track, the jerky electric double-deckers cover almost the entire north coast of the island. Enter at the back of the tram, and try to get a seat in the front of the upper deck for the best views of Hong Kong's colourful streets, always crowded with shoppers and nonstop day-and-night activity. You'll pass through Wan Chai, where the world of Suzie Wong once existed, and travel all the way to the eastern extremity of Shau Kei Wan, once a pirates' hangout, and still with a colony of 'boat people' who live on junks and sampans moored in the bay.

The western terminus is in Kennedy Town, an overcrowded section of the city, named after a 19th-century Hong Kong governor, Sir Arthur Kennedy. When you're ready to get off the tram, just drop your HK$2 fare in the box at the front beside the driver.

visiting tycoon, an act that incensed the colonial authorities, who felt that they had the sole right to issue such a 21-gun welcome. As a result, the merchants were forced to limit their salvoes to one a day – and from then on, they signalled the noon hour daily for all to hear. The gun was made famous by Noel Coward's satirical song, *Mad Dogs and Englishmen*.

Farther east is Hong Kong's largest park, **Victoria Park**, with sports grounds, swimming pool and gardens. On the eastern side of the park on Causeway Road is **Tin Hau Temple**, dedicated to Tin Hau, the Taoist Queen of Heaven and patroness of seafarers. Originally the temple was on the shore, but reclamation projects have now left it high and dry. On the 23rd day of the Third Moon, the birthday of the goddess is celebrated here and in all Hong Kong fishing communities.

Typhoon Alert

No natural danger poses more of a threat to Hong Kong than a typhoon (*dai fung* or 'big wind' in Cantonese). Typhoons always cause damage, and some disastrous ones have occurred throughout Hong Kong's history. However, although Hong Kong gets around five or more typhoons every year, it is usually spared a direct hit and fatalities are now rare.

Typhoons generally occur between July and September. A series of signals from one to ten alerts residents in the event of a storm. Signal No. 1 goes up when a tropical storm that could escalate into a typhoon has moved within a 740-km (460-mile) radius of Hong Kong. People generally pay little attention at this point. Signal 3 means that the winds have escalated, accompanied, perhaps, by heavy rains. Tours and harbour cruises are suspended, and some businesses close.

No. 8 is more serious: it means that the gale has reached Hong Kong. Banks, offices, museums and most shops and restaurants close, and local transport and flights are disrupted. In case of a No. 8 warning, you should remain in your hotel and check the storm's progress on TV or radio.

A night at the Happy Valley races

At the eastern end of Hong Kong Island, past North Point and Quarry Bay, and best reached on foot (15 minutes) from Shau Kei Wan MTR station, is the **Hong Kong Museum of Coastal Defence** (open Fri–Wed 10am–5pm; admission fee). Housed in the restored Lei Yue Mun Fort, which was built by the British, it showcases 600 years of coastal defence in southern China, from the Ming dynasty to the 1997 handover. Included are informative videos and displays on the Opium Wars and the Japanese invasion of Hong Kong in 1941.

Happy Valley

Inland from the bay is **Happy Valley**. At one time this was a very miserable valley, a swampland conducive only to breeding malarial mosquitoes. It is now home to Hong Kong's first racecourse. Hong Kong's gamblers are so eager to play the horses that, despite the opening of a bigger and better racecourse at Sha Tin, the **Happy Valley Racecourse** is thriving.

Jumbo Floating Restaurant in Aberdeen harbour

Be sure to visit the **Hong Kong Racing Museum** (open Tues–Sun 10am–5pm; race days 10am–12.30pm; free), which traces the history of the sport.

Aberdeen

Aberdeen is the island's oldest settlement. Once a pirate lair, it is now home to the 'floating population' – the 'boat people' who spend their entire lives on the junks in the harbour, some proudly claiming never to have set foot on land (except for funerals, which don't count). The majority of the 'boat people' have moved to nearby highrises but a sizeable seaborne community remains. The junks are a picturesque sight: children frolicking on the poop deck, women preparing food or playing mahjong, elderly folk watching the sunset, dogs and cats underfoot, songbirds in bamboo cages overhead – and all afloat. The boats may appear deceptively primitive, but many of them have their own electric generators and all the conveniences of modern housing. You can take a tour of the port in one of the small *sampan*. A half-hour tour costs around HK$60 (pay at the end and negotiate a discount for two or more people).

Aberdeen's delightfully gaudy **Jumbo Floating Restaurant** has featured in many a movie set in Hong Kong. Revamped and rebranded as Jumbo Kingdom, it is well worth boarding the free shuttle (Mon–Sat 11am–11.30pm, Sun and public holidays 7am–11.30pm) across the harbour to explore and eat. There's a seafood exhibition on the ground floor, a Chinese restaurant on the second floor and an excellent top deck with al fresco international dining, seafood and great views.

Ocean Park

Ocean Park (open 10am–6pm; admission fee) has over 40 attractions, including gut-turning rides and roller-coasters, Grand Prix go-carts, and an oceanarium with dolphins, sea lions, seals and penguins. It is divided into two areas: Headland and Lowland, linked by a cable car system that offers spectacular views over the South China Sea. The top attractions are two pairs of bamboo-munching pandas: An An and Jia Jia and youngsters Le Le and Ying Ying. The atoll reef with layers of sea life and the shark tunnel are also crowd pleasers. In response to new competition from Disneyland, Ocean Park successfully reinvented itself and attracts record numbers of visitors. Two major new areas will open by 2010: The Waterfront and The Summit.

Cable cars at Ocean Park

Repulse Bay

Continuing around the coast in a counter-clockwise direction, Deep Water Bay offers a good beach and harbours. The next inlet is **Repulse Bay**, a roomy, sandy crescent backed by green hills and always busy with daytrippers. Notice the massive wall of condominiums, built in the 1980s. Apparently the developers left the space in the middle for good *feng shui* – to enable the mountain's 'dragon spirit' to retain access to the sea.

Stanley

Stanley was once one of the main fishing villages on Hong Kong Island. The well-known **Stanley Market** (10am–6pm) is a major source for bargain clothing and other merchandise. The waterfront is lined with restaurants and bars, many of them with balconies offering sea views. A few minutes walk along the bay are modern **Stanley Plaza** shopping mall and historic **Murray House**. The latter was built in Central in 1844, dismantled in 1982, and rebuilt here in 1999. The **Hong Kong Maritime Museum** (open Tues–Fri and Sun 10am–6pm, Sat 10am–7pm; admission fee) on the ground floor tells the story of shipping in Hong Kong.

Feng shui principles brought to bear in Repulse Bay

Shek O

Further along the coast, on the eastern side of the island, is **Shek O**, a seaside village with narrow winding streets, a decent beach and some good restaurants. There are great walks into the surrounding hills, and the beach gets packed out on sunny weekends with local families enjoying BBQs.

The Hong Kong Cultural Centre in Kowloon

KOWLOON

Though much smaller than Hong Kong Island, Kowloon has almost twice the population. In many areas, the density reaches 150,000 inhabitants per square kilometre (a quarter of a square mile). Most of the area's attractions are centered near the tip of the peninsula in the **Tsim Sha Tsui** district. Next to the Star Ferry terminal is **Ocean Terminal**, where international cruise ships dock, and **Harbour City**, a complex of malls, hotels and restaurants. A large reclamation project west of Tsim Sha Tsui is home to the new **International Commerce Centre**, which at 484 metres (1,588ft) will supersede Two IFC as Hong Kong's tallest building when it is completed in 2010.

Waterfront

If you walk east on the Star Ferry terminal concourse, you will find yourself on the **Tsim Sha Tsui Waterfront Promenade**, which begins at the **Clock Tower**, all that remains of the once grand Kowloon-Canton Railway Terminus, which was pulled down in 1975 and replaced by a modern building in Hung Hom. Don't rely on the clock tower times: the four clocks on the faces of the tower are not synchronised.

The promenade offers unparalled views of the harbour and Hong Kong Island. **The Avenue of Stars**, Hong Kong's version of the Hollywood Walk of Fame is here – a star-studded path that honours those involved in the territory's film industry. Few of the names will be familiar to non-locals, but you'll recognise Bruce Lee, Chow Yun Fat and Jackie Chan.

Flanked by the clock tower is the imposing **Hong Kong Cultural Centre**. Hong Kong's major venue for the performing arts, the building has been criticised for its fortress-like architecture and windowless façade on a site which enjoys one of the most magnificent views in the world. The interior is a comfort-

The Avenue of the Stars, with a view across to Central

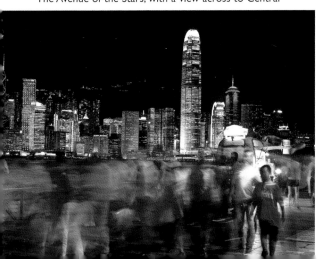

able amalgam of Chinese and Western design, with an impressive main lobby. There are two large concert halls, frequently used by the Hong Kong Philharmonic Orchestra, and a studio theatre, plus a library, an exhibition gallery, shops, restaurants and bars.

Stroll on the prom

A stroll along the TST Waterfront Promenade should be done at least twice during any stay in Hong Kong, once by day and once by night. And if you're in Hong Kong for Chinese New Year, this is the place to be to see the fireworks bursting across the city.

Museums

Next door is the **Hong Kong Space Museum** (open Mon, Wed–Fri 1–9pm; Sat–Sun 10am–9pm; admission fee; separate admission to theatre). Its futuristic dome design is striking; inside are interactive exhibits, including one in which you can experience weightlessness. The theatre presents 'sky shows' and IMAX films.

The **Hong Kong Museum of Art** (open Fri–Wed, 10am–6pm; admission fee) stands behind the Space Museum next to the cultural centre. It contains the Xubaizhi collection of painting and calligraphy; galleries devoted to antiquities and ceramics; and a gallery of work by artists from the contemporary Hong Kong School. Also of interest is the collection of paintings and photographs of old Hong Kong.

A few blocks up Chatham Road South are two more major museums. The **Hong Kong Science Museum** (open Mon–Wed, Fri 1–9pm, Sat–Sun 10am–9pm; admission fee) is a state-of-the-art interactive museum that will teach you how everything and anything works, from ancient sailing ships to the latest technology. The **Hong Kong Museum of History** (open Mon, Wed–Sat 10am–6pm, Sun 10am–7pm; admission fee) opened its new permanent exhibition *The Hong Kong Story* in 2001, with spectacular interactive exhibits showcasing 6,000 years of Hong Kong's history and cultural heritage.

Peninsula Hotel

Located just across Salisbury Road from the cultural centre is the historic hotel, **The Peninsula Hong Kong**, now expanded and modernised by a 32-storey tower *(see page 133)*. Opened in 1928, The Peninsula was the first hotel on Kowloon, strategically positioned for passengers travelling overland to Europe by train. The lobby became the favourite rendezvous for high society, and to this day, guests sit beneath the restored gilt stucco ceiling to see and be seen. Afternoon high tea or evening cocktails to strains of the resident string orchestra are a wonderful way for visitors to recapture the atmosphere of a bygone age, but do pay attention to your attire.

Nathan Road

Alongside the hotel runs busy **Nathan Road**, Hong Kong's fabled shopping street, lined with shops, hotels and restau-

The lights of Kowloon's Nathan Road

rants. Kowloon's main street was created by Sir Matthew Nathan when he was governor of Hong Kong at the turn of the 19th century. When it was constructed, many thought it absurd to have a tree-lined boulevard running through what was practically wilderness. Now the former 'Nathan's Folly' is known as the 'Golden Mile'.

A few blocks up Nathan Road is **Kowloon Park** (open daily 6am–midnight), elegantly laid out with fountains, promenades and ornamental gardens; be sure to go up the steps to see the Sculpture Walk, where artists from Hong Kong and other countries exhibit their works of art. The mosque in the southeast corner of Kowloon Park is the largest in the territory with three storeys and four minarets. Hong Kong has around 80,000 Muslims. Further up Nathan Street is **Yau Ma Tei**, one of the older parts of Kowloon. Turn off Nathan and walk down Kansu Street to find the **Jade Market** (open 9am–6pm), with more than 100 stalls spread out in a large tent, just before you reach the overpass.

Temple Street Night Market

Hong Kong's liveliest market scene is the **Temple Street Night Market** (open 4pm–midnight), near Jordan Road. Everything is sold here, from clothing to souvenirs to electronic goods, and bargaining is an intrinsic part of the shopping experience. The market is known for its pavement food stalls, where you can dine inexpensively on seafood.

The market runs all the way up to **Tin Hau Temple**, where you will find fortune tellers' tables (some speak English) and possibly street performers singing Chinese opera (or pop songs). The temple is one of many in Hong Kong dedicated to Tin Hau, goddess of seafarers; this one also houses an altar to Shing Wong, the city's god. In the daytime the temple (open 8am–6pm) attracts worshippers, while its park attracts strollers and mahjong players.

Yuen Po Street Bird Garden

Nathan Road goes all the way up to **Boundary Street**, which marks the border between Kowloon and the New Territories. Near Boundary Street, off Prince Edward Street West, is the **Yuen Po Street Bird Garden** (open 8am–7pm). Songbirds are popular pets in Chinese households; their owners take them for walks every day, carrying the cages through the streets. Here, the birds entertain passers-by with a symphony of shrill arias; as well as birds, you will find intricately-made cages for sale.

Further north in Sham Shui Po, west of the junction of Nathan Road and Boundary Street, is the **Lei Cheng Uk Han Tomb and Museum** on Tonkin Street (open Mon–Wed, Fri–Sat 10am–1pm, 2–6pm, Sun 1–6pm). This ancient burial vault is believed to date back to the Han Dynasty (AD25–220). The barrel-vaulted chambers were discovered during excavations for a nearby housing development.

Wong Tai Sin

One of Hong Kong's brightest, biggest and busiest temples is the Sik Sik Yuen **Wong Tai Sin Temple** in central Kowloon. It is dedicated to a shepherd boy from Zhejiang who had special healing powers and came to be revered as a demi-god after his death. The incense-wreathed temple complex, which has halls dedicated to the Taoist, Confucian and Buddhist faiths, is especially packed out at Lunar New Year with locals praying for prosperity and rattling fortune sticks.

In the Bird Garden

A picturesque bay on the Sai Kung peninsula

NEW TERRITORIES

Hong Kong's New Territories begin at Boundary Street in Prince Edward. Surprises spring up on all sides: industrial complexes alongside sleepy farming villages, skyscraper towns in the middle of nowhere, Hakka women in traditional flat straw hats, water buffalo and azaleas everywhere. The area can be explored via buses, the MTR and the **Kowloon-Canton Railway** (now part of the MTR system). One line runs north from Tsim Sha Tsui East to Sha Tin and on to the Lo Wu terminus at the Chinese border. Another line gives access to the western New Territories. The HKTB's Land Between and Heritage tours are good ways to cover a lot of ground in a short time.

Tsuen Wan

The main highway makes a circuit of the New Territories, beginning with the new town of **Tsuen Wan**, situated in an area of heavy industry just west of Kowloon. Set amid Tsuen Wan's residential towers, a short walk from the MTR station, is the 18th-century walled village of **Sam Tung Uk**. Built by a Chan clan in 1786, it is now preserved as a museum (open Wed–Mon, 9am–5pm; free). On display is period furniture and farming implements, as well as exhibitions on Chinese folk culture.

North of the town, a commanding view over the New Territories can be seen from **Tai Mo Shan**, Hong Kong's highest peak at 957m (3,140ft). The highway continues parallel to the coast. One-third of all Hong Kong's beaches are to be found in a single 14-km (9-mile) stretch of this region's shoreline. Place names are often based on the distance to the nearest mile-post, as measured from the tip of the Kowloon peninsula. Thus you will find '19½ mile Beach' at Castle Peak Bay.

Tuen Mun

Not far from Tsuen Wan, at milepost 21 near the large new town of Tuen Mun, is a Taoist retreat known as **Ching Chung Koon**. This 'Temple of Green Pines' is a spacious complex containing temples and pavilions, as well as statues and gardens. It is known for its collection of bonsai and houses a jade seal more than 1,000 years old. Among the ponds is one inhabited by turtles: visitors toss in coins in the hope of bouncing one off a turtle's head as a way of achieving good fortune.

A slower pace of life after the bustle of Hong Kong

Temple courtyard at Ching Chung Koon

Hong Kong Wetland Park

North of Tuen Mun, the **Hong Kong Wetland Park** (open Wed–Mon 10am–5pm) covers an area of 61 hectares (151 acres), and shows the diversity of Hong Kong's wetland ecosystem. The park is sandwiched between the high rises of Tin Shui Wai and Shenzhen across the border. Circular walks meander through the wetlands and there are hides with telescopes for bird watching. Almost 130 bird species have been recorded at the park, including varieties of egret and heron, and the rare black-faced spoonbill.

Walled Villages

An extremely interesting image from Chinese history is the walled village of **Kat Hing Wai**, in the village of Kam Tin just outside the market town of Yuen Long. This is the most easily accessible of the New Territories' walled villages. The village is built in a square, and the only way in is through

Tang Chung Ling Ancestral Hall

the gate in the brick defensive wall. Kat Hing Wai was built four or five centuries ago by the Hakka Tang clan, one of the Five Great Clans that migrated here from North China *(see page 11)*. Many of the old houses in the village have been replaced by modern structures.

The Tang clan's earliest walled village was **Lo Wai**, which also has its defensive wall intact. Adjacent to the village is the restored **Tang Chung Ling Ancestral Hall** (open Wed–Mon 9am–1pm and 2–5pm), which dates from the early 16th century. Few traditional ancestral halls remain in China since the anti-historical destruction during the Cultural Revolution, so these New Territories ancestral halls are rare survivors. Another such hall, belonging to the Liu Clan, is Liu Man Shek Tong in the village of Sheung Shui.

Tai Fu Tai

One of the most interesting sites in the New Territories is **Tai Fu Tai** (open Wed–Mon 9am–1pm and 2–5pm), in San Tin, a mansion that belonged to a Confucian high official. The house was built in 1865 by a member of the Man clan who achieved the rank of *tai fu* (mandarin) by doing well in the Imperial Examinations. The traditional Qing Dynasty style of the recently-restored mansion is enlivened by a few Western touches: a Baroque-style ceiling and stained glass above the doorways, showing the builder's modern attitude at the time of construction.

Window on China

The main road continues clockwise around the New Territories. As you approach the border, you can see the skyscrapers of **Shenzhen**, one of China's most successful Special Economic Zones, but whose main attraction for tourists is its cheap shopping *(see page 75)*. The lookout point at Lok Ma Chau was once known as Hong Kong's 'window on China'. In the years of China's isolation from the West, tourists would come to the lookout point here to get a glimpse of the great mystery beyond.

Sha Tin

Continuing around the main road back towards Tsuen Wan you'll come to **Sha Tin**, the site of the **Man Fat Tze**, also known as the Monastery of 10,000 Buddhas, set on a hillside above a vast spread of housing blocks. There are hundreds of stone steps to walk up before you reach the monastery with its regiments of small gilt statues of Buddha (no less than 12,800 of them) lining the walls. The monastery was founded in 1957 by the monk Yuet Kai, who died in 1965 at the age of

Make a Wish

If you need to change your luck, visit the Wishing Tree in the lush valley of Lam Tsuen, near Tai Po in the New Territories. There are actually two wishing trees; the desiccated one, struck by lightning, is purported to be the real wishing tree, but the one near the road, a large banyan, is prettier. In any case, from the nearby temple you can secure an orange tied to swatches of red paper. Write your wishes on the paper, and see how high you can throw your orange into the tree. The higher it goes, the more chance you have of your wish coming true. However, after a branch gave way in 2005, visitors are encouraged to leave their wishes on a nearby rack while the banyan tree regenerates.

The nine-storey pagoda at the Temple of 10,000 Buddhas

87. He had previously predicted that his body would not decompose if he were to be buried behind the temple in a crouching position. True enough, when his disciples exhumed the body eight months later, they found it still in good condition. They covered his corpse in gold leaf and placed it in a building on the second level. It is possible to climb to the top of the nine-storey pink pagoda for a panoramic view.

Also located in Sha Tin, by the Shing Mun River Channel, is the **Hong Kong Heritage Museum** (open Mon, Wed–Sat 10am–6pm, Sun 10am–7pm; admission fee). The museum contains a fun interactive guide to Cantonese opera, art galleries showing work from all over Asia as well as exhibits dedicated to telling the story of Hong Kong's culture and history.

Down to earth, the **Sha Tin Racecourse** can accommodate more than 80,000 spectators and is equipped with every imaginable luxury, including a giant video screen facing the stands, and for the horses, air-conditioned stables. Opposite the Sha Tin railway station, **New Town Plaza** features shops, cinemas and even a computer-controlled musical fountain.

At University station, north of Sha Tin, the modern campus of the **Chinese University of Hong Kong** is visible. The **Art Museum** (open 10am–5pm; free) in the Institute of Chinese Studies Building is worth a visit for its painting and calligraphy collections.

Two rock formations are always pointed out on excursions. Sha Tin Rock, better known as **Amah (Mother) Rock**, is actually a pile of several rocks that resemble a woman with a baby in a sling on her back. Legend has it that a local woman climbed the hill every day to watch for her husband returning from across the sea; one day the wife and her child were turned to stone as a permanent symbol of her enduring faith. Closer to town is **Lion Rock**, shaped like a lion lying in wait.

Sai Kung

The **Sai Kung Peninsula**, to the east of Sha Tin, is the location of two official parks and nature preserves. The south side of the peninsula is the place to go to find some of the territory's best beaches. **Sai Kung** town itself is a pretty seaside village with a resort-like atmosphere. There are good seafood restaurants and a promenade where you can watch the fishermen sell their catch from their small craft.

Wild and Beautiful

Remote areas of the New Territories and sections of Lantau Island are happy sighting grounds for birdwatchers. Hundreds of species have been recorded, from everyday egrets and funny-faced cockatoos to mynahs and pelicans. The Sai Kung Peninsula Nature Preserve has many hiking trails for the nature lover.

As civilisation encroaches, wild animals have been vanishing: leopards have not been seen in 20 years. But you can still come across barking deer, monkeys, porcupines and scaly anteaters. In the wilderness you may also stumble upon a banded krait, a cobra, or some other fearsome snake. Though sightings are common, bitings are rare.

A Dragon Boat in Silvermine Bay, Lantau

OUTLYING ISLANDS

In the waters around Hong Kong there are over 235 outlying islands. Many are uninhabited or home to very small communities. The major islands of Lantau, Cheung Chau and Lamma are full of fascinating contrasts and it is worth setting aside a couple of half days to visit. Start your exploration on the Hong Kong Island waterfront, at the Outlying Islands Ferry Piers in front of the IFC, and catch one of the cheap and reasonably comfortable ferries used by the islanders themselves. For ferry information, *see page 120*.

Getting to Lantau

Lantau can be reached by road and MTR, as well as by ferry. Visitors to Disneyland can take the special MTR Disneyland Resort line, which runs for 3.5km between Sunny Bay and the Disneyland Resort terminus, aboard special Disney-themed trains.

Lantau

Ferries depart from Central Pier 6 at least every hour from 6.10am until late at night to **Mui Wo (Silvermine Bay)**, where you can catch buses to all parts of the island.

Lantau is not as tranquil as it once was. In the 1990s Hong Kong International Airport opened at Chek Lap Kok on the northwest coast, a new town was built at Tung Chung, and the Tsing Ma road-rail bridge connected Lantau to the New Territories. Hong Kong Disneyland Resort has also brought millions more visitors. Yet much of the island remains rural, with more than half of it protected parkland. There is a 69-km (43-mile) circular hiking trail *(see page 90)*. At 934m (3,064-ft), **Lantau Peak** is high enough to attract the occasional rain cloud – cool breezes blow on most hot days.

Visitors intending to include a beach in their itinerary should head for **Cheung Sha Beach**, 3km (2 miles) long and popular for its beautiful white sand and excellent facilities.

Lantau's most famous site is the world's tallest seated bronze statue of Buddha, the 22-m (73-ft) **Tiantan Buddha**. The statue is perched on a peak, up 268 steps, above **Po Lin Monastery** (open daily 10am–6pm; vegetarian lunch, noon–4pm), set in central Lantau's glorious upland scenery. Note that the monastery is strictly vegetarian and visitors are warned not to bring any meat with them.

Close to Po Lin is the beautifully landscaped village of **Ngong Ping** (<www.np 360.com.hk>), a Buddhist

The giant Tiantan Buddha at Po Lin Monastery

The fishing harbour at Tai O

theme park, where you'll find traditional Chinese teashops and two multimedia theatres telling the story of Buddha.

From high-rise Tung Chung, travel through the hills by road to the pretty fishing village at **Tai O**. The Kwan Tai temple here dates back to 1530. Many villagers are descended from Tanka 'fishing' people and live in stilt houses above the water. Tai O is a good place to try to spot Hong Kong's endangered pink dolphins, and the village is also home to the Hong Kong Shaolin Wushu Centre (<www.shaolincc.hk>), which promotes the traditional Chinese martial art.

Lantau's mountains provide a stunning backdrop to **Hong Kong Disneyland** (open daily; park hours, show and firework display times change regularly, see <www.hongkong disneyland.com>). There are two hotels: Disney's Hollywood Hotel and the Victorian-style Hong Kong Disneyland Hotel, which offer good views of Hong Kong and up-close views of the nightly fireworks.

The resort's attractions and layout are similar to other locations in Paris, Tokyo and the US, though the park is smaller. It is divided into different themed areas: the nostalgic Main Street USA evokes a typical small town in the American mid-west from the early 1900s, complete with marching bands; Fantasyland is set around a fairy-tale castle where stories and characters such as Winnie the Pooh, Dumbo and Snow White are brought to life; Adventureland is billed as 'an exotic trek into unexplored regions', with attractions including a Jungle River Cruise and Tarzan's Treehouse; and Tomorrowland focuses on space exploration, featuring a dramatic roller-coaster, a Buzz Lightyear extravaganza and other extraterrestrial thrills.

Cheung Chau

Some 10km (6 miles) west of Hong Kong lies the small, crowded island of **Cheung Chau**, only around one square mile in size. More than 25,000 people live here, many of them by fishing, but there is also an expat community, attracted by the laid-back Mediterranean ambience. The island has a checkered past of smuggling and piracy. That era is gone now, but other elements of the island's old life are preserved.

Cheung Chau becomes the centre of Hong Kong life once a year, usually in May, during the **Bun Festival**, a folklore extravaganza *(see page 93)*. For the rest of the year, life goes on at its accustomed pace: rickety machines chugging in two-man factories, children in school uniforms being ferried home to houseboats and elderly fishermen stirring shrimp paste.

Buns for the Bun Festival

Pak Tai temple on Cheung Chau

By way of formal attractions, **Pak Tai Temple**, built in 1783, has some fine carvings and a great iron sword said to be 600 years old. Pak Tai means 'Ruler of the North' and he is usually represented in a sitting position, with his feet resting on a tortoise and a snake. The statue of Pak Tai is credited with saving the village from a plague that struck Cheung Chau in the 18th century.

From the main township of **Cheung Chau** it's possible to take a walk via the harbour road (15 minutes) or the scenic Peak Road (45 minutes) to the village of **San Wai**, which has a temple dedicated to Tin Hau, goddess of the sea and protectress of fisherfolk. You can also take a *kai do*, or water taxi from the pier next to the ferry pier.

The **Praya**, the promenade in front of the ferry pier, is a good place to observe the many junks and fishing boats in the harbour. There are also several open-air restaurants where you can enjoy fresh seafood. At the other side of the island, at the end of Tung Wan Road, is the popular **Tung Wan Beach**. Further along the headland is Kwun Yam Wan beach, where you can rent boards from the windsurfing centre.

Lamma

Less than 30 minutes by fast ferry from Central, sleepy Lamma Island is perfect for swimming, hiking, picnicking, birdwatching, or just relaxing. Hong Kong's third largest island has a population of only about 12,000; it is still largely undeveloped and has a laid-back atmosphere. Archaeologists believe that Lamma has probably been inhabited for some 4,000 years and the island is known as 'Hong Kong's Stone Age Island'.

Try and plan a trip during a weekday, as Lamma tends to be swamped by daytrippers at the weekend. The principal settlements on the island are **Yung Shue Wan** on Lamma's northwest coast and **Sok Kwu Wan** on the east coast. Both villages offer good waterfront restaurants with Cantonese seafood fresh from the tank. The ports are within hiking distance of several beautiful beaches and within a one-hour hike of each other on a marked trail. You can build up an appetite for dinner by making your way from the beach to the restaurant. Yung Shue Wan is a very international enclave, with many boisterous pubs, plus vegetarian, Japanese, Thai, Indian, Italian and Turkish, as well as Chinese restaurants.

Laid-back Lamma is a 35-minute ferry ride from Central

EXCURSION TO MACAU

Macau, the final bastion of Portugal's great 16th-century empire, is much more than just a quirk of history. Here, where East and West first met, parts of the enclave still beautifully combine a taste of Asia with something of the sunny atmosphere of the Mediterranean. In its 21st-century incarnation, Macau has also taken on some of the exuberance of Las Vegas, thanks to the excitement that the new casino developments and booming visitor numbers have generated.

Macau's historic centre, the Largo do Senado, with its colonial architecture, has a distinctly Mediterranean flavour. Colonnaded public buildings, iron balconies, winding streets, flagstoned squares and the many churches all speak of the Portuguese inheritance as well as the Chinese, a fusion of East and West that has produced the unique Macanese culture.

The story of the European discovery of Macau begins in 1513, when Portuguese explorer Jorge Alvares reached the south coast of China. Traders followed in his wake, setting up bases in several parts of the Pearl River estuary. Finally, in 1557, they were all consolidated in Macau. It was the only European gateway to China, and through it flowed Western technology and religion. In 1576, Pope Gregory XIII created the Macau diocese, which covered all of China and Japan.

The location presented significant trade opportunities for its possessors. As China and Japan were not on speaking terms, trade between them had to be channelled through a neutral middleman and lucky Macau was ideal for the job. Portugal's resulting near-monopoly of East–West trade understandably awakened the competitive instincts of other European powers. The Dutch sent an invasion flotilla to Macau in 1622, but the defenders triumphed. However, the end of

The remaining façade of the ruined St Paul's Church, Macau

the golden age was drawing near. China began to relax trade restrictions, and with the rise of Hong Kong, Macau became an isolated Portuguese outpost.

In the 17th century Macau provided a haven for persecuted Japanese Christians, and during World War II Portugal's neutrality brought the territory a new flood of refugees. They were joined by a swarm of spies of all conceivable nationalities, and Macau won a name for international intrigue.

The territory was formally handed back to China in 1999. Now known as the Macau Special Administrative Region (MSAR), it is governed under a 'one country, two

Getting to and Around Macau

The easiest way to get to Macau is by TurboJET ferry (tel: 2921 6688). Jetfoils run every 15 to 30 minutes, 24 hours a day from the Macau Ferry Terminal at the Shun Tak Centre in Sheung Wan, just west of the Central ferry piers. The fare is around HK$155 and the trip to Macau's main ferry terminal takes about an hour. There are also four departures daily from the Sky Pier near the Hong Kong International Airport (45 minutes; HK$180).

Cotai Jet Ferries (tel: 2859 1588) run hourly services between 7am and 5pm from the Shun Tak Centre to a new pier in Macau on Taipa island. This will hopefully ease congestion at Macau's main terminal.

The Macau Government Tourist Office at 336–7 Shun Tak Centre (tel: 2857 2287) can assist with information. Most nationalities need only a passport to enter Macau. The *pataca*, Macau's own currency, is pegged to the Hong Kong dollar, and you can use your Hong Kong currency in Macau.

There is another Macau Government Tourist Office at the main ferry terminal in Macau. Outside, there are free shuttle buses to hotels and casinos, as well as taxis, pedicabs and mini-buses to all points (take 3, 3A, 10, or 10A to the historic centre; exact change required). Pedicabs (tricycles carrying two passengers) were once Macau's most common form of transport, but in today's traffic their attraction is diminishing.

systems' set-up, similar to that in Hong Kong.

Over the past 10 years the region's landscape has changed significantly, primarily as a result of the opening up of the MSAR's gaming industry. Ambitious reclamation has created new land (known as the NAPE zone) on the Macau peninsula's Porto Exterior (Outer Harbour) and, most dramatically, the islands of Coloane and Taipa have been joined by reclaimed land now called the Cotai strip. Macau is the only place in Greater China where gaming is legal; Chinese people love to bet and are travelling in ever increasing numbers. The arrival of Nevada-style casinos has transformed Macau into Asia's Las Vegas and the tiny enclave now earns more money from gaming than the Las Vegas Strip itself.

Traditional Macau pedicab

Sights in Macau

If you arrive from Hong Kong, The Sands casino in the outer harbour is one of the first sights you'll see in the 'new Macau'. Just in front of it is the **Fisherman's Wharf** theme park (open 24 hours, rides open 10am–9pm; free admission, fees for rides) where replicas of European buildings, a Tang dynasty palace and an 'active' volcano house fun-fair rides, amusements, shops and restaurants. The grandstand, situated opposite the ferry terminal on **Avenida da Amizade** (Friendship Avenue), marks the finishing line for the Macau Grand Prix, an international car-racing event held here every November.

Tiles in the Leal Senado building

The 'Historic Centre of Macau' was added to the UNESCO World Heritage list in 2005, acknowledging its importance as the place where Eastern and Western culture first met, as well as its unique architectural heritage. Start your exploration at **Largo do Senado** (Senate Square). For an authentic feel of old Portugal, slip into the cool entrance hall of the impressive **Leal Senado** (Loyal Senate) building, a fine example of colonial architecture. First built in 1784, the inside walls are covered in flowered blue tiles *(azulejos)* and coats of arms. An inscription over the archway reads, *'Cidade do nome de Deus, não ha outra mais leal'* ('City of the name of God, none is more loyal') – praise for Macau's loyalty during the Spanish occupation of Portugal in the 17th century, when the enclave refused to fly the aggressor's flag.

Macau's most memorable monument is the baroque façade of the **Ruins of St Paul's** (São Paulo), the only remaining part of a beautiful 17th-century Jesuit church. On top of a hill in the centre of the city, it's approached by a grand staircase. The rest of the building, an adjoining college and the nearby Monte Fortress were destroyed in a fire in 1835. The rich sculptural effects on the facade mix Eastern and Western symbols: familiar saints, Chinese dragons and a Portuguese caravel.

The ambitious **Museum of Macau** (open Tues–Sun 10am–6pm; admission fee) opened in 1998 in the lower levels of

Macau Essentials

Shopping: Like Hong Kong, Macau is a duty-free port. Shops aimed at the tourist market are interspersed with the more workaday ironmongers, herbalists and noodle stalls.

Macau is famous for its gold jewellery. Market prices per *tael* (34g/ 1.2oz) of gold are set daily. You should always ask for a certificate of guarantee when you buy gold or jewellery. Look for jewellery shops along Avenida do Infante D. Henrique and Avenida de Almeida Ribeiro.

Knowledgeable visitors look for antiques – either Chinese heirlooms or remnants from the Portuguese colonial days. Both antiques and excellent reproductions of 18th- and 19th-century Chinese furniture are found in the shops leading up to St Paul's on Rua de São Paolo. The side streets leading off the east side of Largo do Senado have plenty of factory outlet shops selling over-runs and seconds from Macanese and Chinese factories.

Wynn Macau has an arcade packed with international brand names, and at The Venetian Macao you can explore The Grand Canal Shoppes by gondola. Also worth exploring are the Sunday market at Taipa and the small antique and reproduction furniture shops in Coloane village.

Dining: Macau's own cuisine is a combination of Chinese cooking styles and ingredients, infused with flavours imported from Portugal, Brazil and Africa. Whether you choose to dine in one of the Macanese, Chinese, traditional Portuguese, or international-style restaurants, you will be treated to a hearty meal at a good price.

Fresh fish and seafood is particularly good. A delicate, delicious fish is Macau sole *(linguado)*. Imported dried cod *(bacalhao)* is the Portuguese national dish; several varieties are available in local restaurants, usually baked.

Macau has an ample supply of Portuguese wines. Try *vinho verde*, a mildly sparkling young wine from northern Portugal, or a hearty red Dão or Colares. After dinner, a glass of Madeira or port is recommended to round off the meal.

Cannon at Monte Fortress

the **Monte Fortress** (open daily 7am–7pm), which was built by the Jesuits in the 17th century as a defence against the Dutch. Entrance is by an escalator, near St Paul's. The museum gives an overview of Macau's history and traditions.

Luís Vaz de Camões (1524–80), the Portuguese national poet whose work immortalised the country's golden age of discoveries, may have stayed in Macau. Local legend claims that he wrote part of his great saga, *Os Lusíadas*, in what is now called the **Camões Grotto**, situated in the spacious tropical Camões Garden.

Next to the garden, behind a gate (opened to anyone who knocks), is the **Old Protestant Cemetery**. Those whose fate it was to die on some far foreign field could not have wished for a more peaceful, lovely graveyard. The small, white-washed chapel was the first Protestant church built in China.

For a taste of Old China, visit the classic **Lou Lim Ieoc Garden**. Here, arched bridges, pagodas, fish ponds and stands of bamboo create the mood of a timeless Chinese painting. Nearby is the **Memorial House of Dr Sun Yat-sen** (open Wed–Mon 10am–5pm), founder of the Chinese Republic. Photos and documents tell the story of the physician-statesman, who lived for a time in Macau, but never in this building.

Kun Iam Tong, off Avenida do Coronel Mesquita (open daily 8am–6pm), is a 17th-century Buddhist temple of considerable splendour and charm. Surrounded by statues, carvings and incense burners, the faithful make their devotions and check their fortunes, and traditional funerary displays give a cheerful send-off to the recently departed. An unexpected piece of historical memorabilia turns up in the monastery garden, where guides point out a small stone table used for a treaty-signing ceremony in 1844. The signatories, who were the Chinese viceroy from Canton and the minister plenipotentiary of the United States of America, put their names to a historic document – the first-ever treaty between the two countries.

On NAPE, a swathe of reclaimed land southwest of the ferry terminal, is the **Macau Cultural Centre**, with two auditoria, galleries, a conference hall and dance and music studios. The adjacent **Museum of Art** (open Tues–Sun 10am–6.30pm; admission fee) houses a collection of over 3,000 works. Nearby, dominating the skyline on a small manmade causeway, stands the 20-m (66-ft) bronze **statue of Kun Iam**, sculpted by Portuguese artist Christina Reira.

The 17th-century Buddhist temple of Kun Iam Tong

Underneath, in the dome-shaped lotus, there's a small meditation centre and library.

Further along the shoreline, past the Nam Van Lakes, the **Macau Tower** stretches 338m (1,109ft) above the city. For a fee you can take a lift to the observation tower for panoramic views, and if you are brave you can walk around outside, climb the mast or try bungee jumping. There's a revolving restaurant on top of the tower, and in the adjoining convention centre you'll find a shopping plaza, more restaurants and a cinema.

Macau's oldest museum, the **Maritime Museum** (open Wed–Mon 10am–5.30pm; admission fee) traces the history of Macau's connection to the sea. Exhibits cover fishing, seaborne trade, sea transport, and there is an aquarium. The museum also offers boat tours aboard a fishing junk.

The museum is almost on the spot where the Portuguese first landed. When they came ashore they found the **A-Ma Temple** (properly called Ma Kok Temple; open daily dawn to dusk), dedicated to the favourite goddess of fishermen, who is also known as Tin Hau. The area was called A-Ma Gau ('Bay of A-Ma'), which is the source of Macau's name. The ornate, picturesque temple dates from the Ming Dynasty (1368–1644) and is the oldest building in Macau.

The strategically located **Barra Fortress** once defended the southern tip of the peninsula. Although not completed until 1627, it was instrumental in defending Macau's inner harbour against the 1622 attack by the Dutch. Used only once, the fort's cannons were exchanged for rice to feed World War II refugees. Part of the fortress is now used as a hotel, the Pousada de Sao Tiago, which still contains the original **chapel of Sao Tiago** (St James), a saint much revered in the area.

The northernmost point in Macau is the frontier between two contrasting worlds. The **Barrier Gate** (Portas do Cerco), which was built more than a century ago, marks the boundary between the MSAR and the People's Republic of China.

Casinos

Macau is famous for gambling and the new wave of Las Vegas-style casinos has added some pizzazz to the enclave's main revenue earner. The first of these glamorous newcomers was **Sands Macau**, which has 277 gaming tables and 405 slot machines. Others, like the **Venetian** *(see page 68)*, **Galaxy Casino** and the **Greek Mythology** casino, complete with Roman centurions, offer plenty of spectacle. Kitsch old favourite the **Lisboa** remains popular, it but is now dwarfed by the enormous glistening **Wynn Macau** and MGM Macau, and the preposterous-looking **Grand Lisboa**.

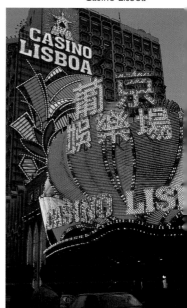

Casino Lisboa

In packed halls, thousands of visitors, mainly Chinese, play the familiar international games – blackjack, craps, roulette, baccarat – or hit the miles of slot machines. The 24-hour casinos have no admission charge and allow fairly casual dress, though men are required to wear long trousers. If you want a change of scene there are always more gambling opportunities available. You can try greyhound-racing at the Canidrome (one of the largest in the world) or horse-racing on Taipa.

Taipa and Coloane

Bridges link Macau to Taipa, which will soon have its own
ferry terminal as well as the Macau International Airport.

The quaint **Taipa Village**, with its narrow lanes and colonial buildings painted yellow, blue and green, has been almost
completely swallowed up by the development of nearby housing estates. Pay a visit to the mint-green **Taipa Houses Museum** (open Tues–Sun 9.30am–5pm; admission fee), where
five beautifully restored buildings house art galleries and museums. The island is also home to the University of East Asia.

The island of **Coloane** is now firmly connected to Taipa
by the Cotai strip, 80 hectares (200 acres) of reclaimed land
dominated by the 40-storey **Venetian Macao Resort Hotel**.
The Venetian has 3,000 rooms, 55,000 sq m (600,000 sq ft)
of casino space, a 15,000 seat sports arena, a 1,500 seat theatre for the likes of Cirque de Solei,l and an indoor life-size

The Macau–Taipa Bridge

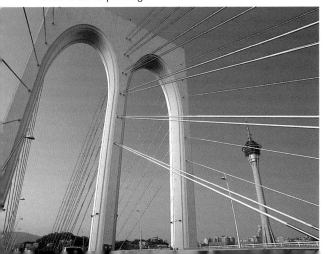

reproduction of St Mark's Square. It will be joined by at least 12 more hotels and casinos before 2010, including the underwater, Atlantis-themed City of Dreams casino.

Once past the temptations of the Cotai strip, Coloane itself remains relatively undeveloped and its main attractions include a country park and beaches. Cheoc Van Beach and Hac Sa Beach ('Black Sands') are both popular resort areas, with lifeguards on duty in summer and windsurfing boards for hire. There are restaurants, swimming pools and changing facilities.

The 170-m (560-ft) peak of Coloane island is marked by a 20-m (65-ft) statue of the goddess A-Ma, which can be seen from the sea, and the **A-Ma Cultural Village** (open daily 8am–6pm), a newly built Qing-dynasty-style complex with temples, bell tower, drum tower, Tian Hou Palace and museum.

The village of Coloane is peaceful and pretty. On the central square, the tiny **Chapel of St Francis Xavier** is dedicated to the 16th-century patron saint of missionaries. Dine at one of the cafés serving Macanese food and take a walk down the recently restored waterfront along Avenida da Republica to the Kun Lam Temple which was built in 1677 and is dedicated to the gods and goddesses of heaven, war, wealth, medicine and carpenters.

EXCURSION TO GUANGZHOU

Guangzhou, previously known to Westerners as Canton, was China's major seaport for 2,000 years and the centre for European traders in the 19th century. The city still maintains its important gateway role. Ever since 1957 the Canton Trade Fair (Chinese Export Commodities Fair) has attracted throngs of international business people every spring and autumn.

Guangzhou, with a population of almost 10 million, straddles the Zhu Jiang, or Pearl River – China's fifth longest – which skirts the city on its western and southern sides and links it to the South China Sea. This waterway accounts for much of the local charm and excitement, as the daily drama of the ferryboats, junks, sampans, freighters – and even small tankers and big gunboats – unfolds right in the centre of town. The river also irrigates the carefully tended surrounding farmlands, creating a lush, subtropical scene. Guangdong Province has some of China's most fertile land, and grows two crops of rice a year, along with vegetables of all kinds.

Guangzhou is determinedly on the move into the modern world. Thanks to rapid urbanisation, the picturesque older sections with their old houses, narrow streets and winding alleyways may not be around for much longer.

Arriving in Guangzhou

There are many package tours to Guangzhou from Hong Kong (see page 112), and this may be the easiest way to visit the city. However, it's also easy to get to Guangzhou by train or ferry. Seven express trains leave daily from the Kowloon-Canton Railway (KCR) Station in Hung Hom, Kowloon, making the trip in less than two hours. Turbojet craft leave the China Hong Kong City (CHKC) terminal twice a day; the journey takes two hours. The China Travel Service operates a bus route to Guangzhou from just outside the Hung Hom train station, you can buy tickets from any CTS office. There's a bus every hour on average and the journey time is around 3 hours.

You will need a visa to enter China (see page 108). Hong Kong currency is widely accepted in Guangzhou, or you can change your currency into RMB (yuan) at any bank or hotel (see page 117). Guangzhou, like Hong Kong, is primarily Cantonese-speaking, but many people also speak Mandarin. English is spoken in hotels and tourist destinations.

If you travel by train, you will arrive at Guangzhou East Station, a large modern complex, which connects with the underground, buses, hotel transfer services and taxis. The station is in the newer business district; nearby is Asia's sixth-tallest building, Citic Plaza, 391m (1,283ft).

Sights in Guangzhou

Yuexiu Park, situated near the Trade Fair in the northern part of the city, is Guangzhou's largest; it covers a hilly 100 hectares (250 acres). The park is landscaped with lakes and gardens. On a hilltop in the park is the **Zhenhailou** (Tower Overlooking the Sea), one of the city's oldest buildings. This five-storey pavilion was built as a memorial to the seven great sea journeys undertaken by the eunuch Zheng He – to East Africa,

Yuexiu, the largest landscaped park in Guangzhou

the Persian Gulf and Java – between 1405 and 1433. Today it contains a fine collection of historical exhibits.

The **Five Rams Statue** stands in the middle of the park. It celebrates the founding of Guangzhou, when five spirits rode their goats down from the celestial realm to present the inhabitants of the city with their very first grains of rice.

Dr Sun Yat-sen's Memorial Hall (open daily 8am–6pm) honours the founder of the Chinese Revolution, flanked by his heroic statue in copper. Dr Sun Yat-sen (1866–1925) began his political career in Canton. This enormous, modern version of a traditional Chinese building, with sweeping blue tile roofs, contains an auditorium big enough to seat 4,700 people. It was built in 1931 with contributions from overseas Chinese.

Guangzhou's most important Buddhist monument is the 1,400-year-old **Liurong Si** (Temple of the Six Banyan Trees) (open daily 8am–5pm). Although the banyan trees that

Sun Yat-sen's Memorial Hall

once flourished here are now no more, the often-restored complex has remained a focus of local Buddhist activities. Golden Buddha statues in several of Buddha's aspects adorn the temples and overlooking them is the 17-storey **Hua Ta**, or Flower Pagoda, a slender relic of the Song dynasty (AD960–1279).

In the early Middle Ages, Canton had a significant Muslim population as a result of its trade with the Middle East. This explains the presence of the Huaisheng Si, or **Huaisheng Mosque** in Guangzhou, reputed to be China's oldest and traditionally dated AD627. Rebuilt in modern times, the mosque serves the small local community of devout Muslims. The modern minaret is known as the **Guang Ta** (Naked Pagoda), in contrast to the Flower Pagoda of the Buddhist Temple of the Six Banyan Trees.

Chen Jia Ci, the Chen Family Temple (open daily 8.30am–5pm), was built in the late 19th century to promote arts and crafts. An architectural wonder, it is itself a beautiful piece of craftsmanship with its sculpture and carved stone balustrades. Porcelain friezes adorn the rooftops and ridgepoles, telling the story of the *Romance of the Three Kingdoms*. Inside is a collection of ceramics, carvings and furniture. There is also a market and a porcelain shop.

Further north off Jiefang Bei Lu is the **Nanyue Wangmu** (Museum of the Western Han; open daily 9am–5.30pm; admission fee), which recreates the tomb of a Han dynasty emperor dating back more than 2,000 years. The tomb was discovered in 1983, when construction workers were clearing the site to build the China Hotel. Exhibits include skeletons of the emperor and his servants and funeral objects such as jade armour and ornaments.

The atmosphere of 19th-century Canton is best evoked on **Shamian Island**, a haunting, nostalgic place on the Pearl River. This small formerly residential island, beautifully shaded by banyan trees, was the home of the closed community of the foreign colony in the era of 'concessions'. Its stately European-style buildings have since been restored, and restaurants and galleries have opened up among the government offices and foreign legations.

A popular optional excursion is an hour's detour to **Guangzhou Zoo** (open daily 8am–5pm; admission fee), founded in 1958. It houses more than 400 animal species, most famous of which is the giant panda, and has an imaginative monkey-shaped mountain behind a moat.

A visit to Guangzhou's open-air market, **Qing Ping**, is not to be missed. The Cantonese have a reputation for eating almost anything, and Qing Ping's meat market was once famous for having dogs, cats, snakes, insects and rare animals on sale, though this is less common now. Stalls also sell Chinese medicine, antiques, songbirds, tropical fish and more everyday food.

Elegant Shamian

Side Trip to Foshan

A popular day-trip from Guangzhou visits the industrial city of **Foshan**, home to over 5 million people and renowned for its handicrafts for more than 1,000 years. Many artisans' workshops have been replaced by factories, but you can visit the 500-year-old **Ancient Nanfeng Kiln**, and the **Foshan Folk Art Studio**, where you can observe workers making Chinese lanterns, carving sculptures, painting scrolls and cutting intricate designs in paper. The Foshan Art Porcelain Factory has traditional designs, but also some attractive modern pieces.

Foshan's most outstanding artistic monument is **Zu Miao**, the Taoist Ancestral Temple, a Sung dynasty establishment rebuilt in the 14th century and well worth visiting. Constructed in wood, brick, stone, ceramic and bronze, this is a work of extravagant beauty, uniting many ancient art forms. The complex contains the oldest wooden stage in China, used by the Wan Fu Tai Chinese opera.

EXCURSION TO SHENZHEN

Shenzhen was China's first Special Economic Zone. Literally created out of farmland, it was set up in the 1970s as the answer to Hong Kong. It has now grown into a metropolis of more than 10 million people, with tightly clustered skyscrapers and some of China's highest grossing industries.

Because Shenzhen is much cheaper than Hong Kong, it is a popular weekend destination for Hong Kong's Chinese, who come to relax, dine in its resorts and play golf. It is even becoming something of a commuter town – an apartment here costs a fraction of what it would in Hong Kong.

Shenzhen is very easy to reach – the KCR commuter train runs throughout the day, the trip taking about 30 minutes from Kowloon Tong station. Visitors need a visa to enter China and must disembark at the border (now called 'boundary') checkpoint, Lo Wu. Ferries make the one-hour trip (7.30am–5.30pm) from the China Ferry Terminal in Kowloon to Shekou on the Natau Peninsula, which is part of the economic zone.

Shenzhen is a premier shopping centre, and much cheaper than Hong Kong. It is known for its inexpensive (but well-made) knock-off designer goods. You can use your Hong Kong dollars here, so there's no need to change currency. Some places take credit cards, but cash is better for bargaining. Just across the border is the huge **Lo Wu City** shopping mall, which is within walking distance. There are other shopping malls nearby.

Shenzhen's main tourist attractions are its enormous theme parks. One of them – **Splendid China** (daily 9am–8pm) – purports to show 'all of China in one day'. It contains elaborate replicas of China's chief monuments in impressive detail, including a scaled-down version of the Great Wall. The 24 **China Folk Culture Villages** represent China's ethnic variety; they feature craftspeople in traditional costumes along with performances of folk-song and dance .

After dark, Shenzhen reverberates with its wild, albeit tawdry, nightlife. Pubs, discos, karaoke lounges and girlie bars abound at **Lo Wu**, near the station, and **Shekou**, a satellite town to the west.

Shopping in Lo Wu City

WHAT TO DO

SHOPPING

While Hong Kong is no longer the bargain shopping destination it once was, there are still some good buys to be had. Since Hong Kong is a duty-free port and charges no sales tax, goods are cheaper here than in their country of manufacture. On photographic equipment, electronic goods and watches, you avoid the luxury tax payable in your home country. Speciality goods and souvenirs, often handmade, come from Hong Kong and elsewhere in China. Custom-made garments by skillful Hong Kong tailors are still much in demand and cost less than elsewhere for comparable garments. Note that alcohol and tobacco are both exceptions to Hong Kong's duty-free regime and are subject to tax.

You'll find that prices are about the same in Hong Kong Central and Kowloon, and somewhat cheaper in Causeway Bay, which caters to local shopping. Large shops on the fashionable thoroughfares tend to be more expensive than smaller 'family' shops tucked away in the side streets.

Stores do not open until 10am or later, but shopping goes on into the evening, up to 10pm or later. Most shops are open seven days a week. Shops in Central are an exception; they generally close at 7pm and are not open on Sunday. The only holiday on which all commerce comes to a halt is the Chinese New Year in January or February.

Large department stores have fixed prices, but elsewhere you should ask for a discount, especially if you buy several items in one shop. Compare prices before you buy. Always ask to see the manufacturer's guarantee when purchasing watch-

The Bun Festival procession on Cheung Chau

Looking for a good buy

es, cameras and audio-visual and electronic equipment. Note that when haggling, the merchant assumes you are prepared to pay cash. If, after making a deal, you try to pay with a credit card, he may then boost the price.

Shipping. Many stores will pack and ship purchases. Ask if automatic free insurance is provided. If the goods are very valuable or fragile, it is a good idea to buy an all-risk insurance for the shipment.

Where to Buy

Major shopping areas are Tsim Sha Tsui in Kowloon, especially along Nathan Road; Central on Hong Kong Island, particularly for upmarket designer goods; Causeway Bay for slightly better prices; and the Hollywood Road area for antiques.

Department stores. Look for Lane Crawford, an upmarket store with branches at Pacific Place, IFC Mall and Harbour City; Wing On, one of the oldest in Hong Kong; Marks and Spencer; and the Japanese stores, Sogo and Seibu.

Malls. Hong Kong is full of giant malls dedicated to shopping, eating and entertainment. Harbour City, just west of the Star Ferry Terminal in Tsim Sha Tsui, is one of the largest; IFC Mall and The Landmark in Central have major designer brands; Pacific Place is Admiralty's biggest; and Times Square in Causeway Bay has 16 floors of spending opportunities. Most top hotels have boutique malls featuring luxury brands.

Factory outlets. Hong Kong's garment factories have moved elsewhere, but there are still plenty of small outlets dotted about the city selling excess stock, samples and factory over-runs. Try Johnston Road in Wan Chai, Fa Yuen Street in Mong Kok and Stanley Market. Pedder Building at 12 Pedder Street, Central has designer outlets.

Markets. Markets are the places to use your bargaining skills. Hong Kong's most famous and colourful market is the **Temple Street Night Market** near the Jordan MTR stop. Every conceivable kind of goods is sold here: clothing, all sorts of electronics, CDs, souvenirs, crafts and jewellery.

Stanley Market in Stanley is located on Hong Kong's southern coast, and is well-known for all kinds of clothing, including silk and cashmere. Bargain, and carefully examine any merchandise you buy here.

The **Jade Market**, on Kansu Street in Yau Ma Tei, is known for both jade and freshwater pearls. This is not the place to make expensive purchases, but it's great for inexpensive gifts. Look out for regular promotions and discounts that are only available to tourists.

Shopping Tips

Be aware that name brands, including electronics, are sometimes fakes, glass may be sold as jade, and that antique you bought may have been made last night. Always ask for a receipt that records information about the item, and if you buy an antique, be sure to get a certificate of authentication. Needless to say, avoid peddlers who approach you in the street.

It is advisable to shop at outlets that are members of the Hong Kong Tourism Board's (HKTB) Quality Tourism Services Scheme, identified by a black Chinese character encircled by a golden letter Q with a small red junk in the bottom left corner. Membership imposes an obligation to maintain standards of both quality and service. For a list of QTS-accredited outlets, pick up a copy of the HKTB's *A Guide to Quality Shops*. Look out for regular VIP promotions and discounts that are only available to tourists.

Fashion Week

In mid-July, Fashion Week brings parades and events to shopping centres around the city.

What to Buy

Antiques. Hollywood Road, which runs from Central to Sheung Wan, is the most famous antiques street in Hong Kong. Look for fine Chinese bronzes, embroidery, lacquerware and porcelain, tomb figures and wood carvings. The experts point out that it is not age alone that determines a Chinese antique's value – the dynasties of the past had their creative ups and downs. For genuine antiques, try Honeychurch Antiques at No. 29 for furniture and silver, Tai Sing Company at 12 Wyndham Street for porcelain and pottery. For fun you can visit the Low Price Shop at No. 47 or the Cat Street crafts stores and flea market.

Brocades and silks. Fabrics from China are a bargain and well worth taking home. Chinese-product department stores stock silk fabrics, silk scarves, finely embroidered blouses, and traditional padded jackets. Chinese Arts and Crafts is at Pacific Place in Central, and in Star House in Tsim Sha Tsui. For fabrics, try Western Market, Morrison Street, in Sheung Wan.

Cameras. Hong Kong is the place to buy some of the world's most advanced photographic equipment, and there are some real bargains around. However, be sure you compare prices and models before buying. Two reliable places to start looking in Central are Photo Scientific, 6 Stanley Street, and Hing Lee Camera Company, 25 Lyndhurst Terrace.

Carpets and rugs. Hong Kong is a mecca for Chinese hand-knotted wool carpets and silk rugs. Hong Kong's stores are usually able to arrange shipment. Caravan at 65 Hollywood Road and the shops in The Silk Road at Ocean Centre, Harbour City in Tsim Sha Tsui are good places to start looking.

China (porcelain). In Hong Kong you can have a plate, or even a whole dinner service, hand-painted to your own design. Factories in Kowloon and the New Territories, producing traditional and modern china, are geared to entertain and instruct visiting tourists; prices are appealing. A good place to go is the Wah Tung China Company in the Grand Marine Industrial Building in Aberdeen. In antiques shops, look for highly valued porcelains from China. Note that because of the duty-free situation, good bargains may be found in European china, including Spode and Wedgwood.

Electronics. The latest gadgets are sometimes available in Hong Kong before anywhere else. Before you begin shopping, pick up HKTB's *A Guide to Quality Shops* and its visitor pack. Prices on electronics are no longer as competitive as they used to be; check prices at home before you buy here. Nathan Road has many electronics shops, but be careful when buying from the individual stores. It's advisable only to enter these shops if you exactly what you want, and to stick to your choice. Don't listen to the salespeople's advice. Fortress and Broadway are two chain electronics stores which are safe to buy from, although a little bit more expensive than the smaller retailers. Also check out Star Computer City in Star House near the Star Ferry terminal in Kowloon.

Traditional Chinese chops

Furniture. The choice ranges from traditional hand-carved Chinese rosewood furniture to well-made reproductions of modern Western styles.

Rattan furniture is highly popular. Hollywood Road has several furniture shops. Queen's Road East in Wan Chai is a furniture manufacturing and retail area.

Jade. 'Good for the health' is just one of the many qualities attributed to these beautiful emerald-green or turquoise stones. Real jade is extremely expensive, and you may be offered counterfeit jade, which looks exactly like the genuine article. Some people say you can test the authenticity by touch – real jade feels smooth and cool. Alternatively, you can shine a lamp on the stone – real jade shows no reflected light. Better still, go shopping with an expert. Kowloon's Jade Market is popular but you are unlikely to pick up any valuable heirlooms here.

Jewellery. Thanks to the duty-free situation, prices in Hong Kong are lower than they are in some other places. You can buy gemstones loose or set, or have them made up to your own design. Popular purchases include diamonds and freshwater pearls. If you do plan to buy jewellery, be sure to If you do plan to buy jewellery, look out for the Q symbol that indicates the dealer has been accredited by the HKTB's Quality Tourism Services Scheme.

Kitchen equipment. Woks and any other gadgets essential for Chinese cookery make good purchases. Department stores sell all sorts of intriguing kitchen equipment.

Tailoring

Tailor-made clothes are not as popular in Hong Kong as they were, but many shops still remain. Local tailors are experts when it comes to producing custom-made garments for both men and women, and are also adept at copying patterns. The result can be a quality suit at a fair price – but made-to-measure clothing is not cheap. Many tailors are located around Nathan Road and Mody Road in Tsim Sha Tsui. Tai Pan Row Tailors in IFC Mall and at 48 Queen's Road is a respected tailor in Central.

Chinese-style clothes for sale in Hong Kong's malls

Leather goods. Leather is not a great bargain in Hong Kong. Locally made items do not live up to their European models. However, the industry is growing, and there is a wide range of locally produced leather accessories, all at extremely attractive prices. For European imports, you will pay top dollar.

Musical, audio and video equipment. Hong Kong has a vast range of the most high-tech audio-visual, sound, and screen equipment. Before purchasing, visitors should make sure of compatibility with systems in their own countries. Be sure to look around and compare before buying. Whatever you buy, you may be able to gain a discount.

Clothes. Hong Kong's shops carry almost every recognisable European and American label, from top-end designers to the moderately priced or trendy. Nathan Road in Tsim Sha Tsui, Central's shopping malls and Causeway Bay are good places to look. There are still many factory outlet stores, particularly in Wan Chai and Causeway Bay, with reasonable prices.

Temple Street market, Ladies' market in Mong Kok and the Lanes in Central sell cheap Chinese-style clothes.

Tea. Chinese department stores sell gift tins of exotic blends. If you want to learn something about tea, go to the Moon Garden Tea House at 5 Hoi Ping Road, Causeway Bay. The owners will brew up a pot so you can taste before making a choice. The HKTB runs free tea appreciation classes at the Lock Cha Tea Shop in Hong Kong Park on Mondays and Thursdays. You must book the free lesson with the HKTB first.

Watches. The saying 'Time is money' is quite literally true in Hong Kong. An enormous variety of watch makes and models are on sale. Be sure to get the manufacturer's guarantee stamped or signed if you buy a watch. There are plenty of cheap, counterfeit watches for sale in the tourist markets.

ENTERTAINMENT

Hong Kong is a city that never sleeps; plenty of bars and eating places stay open into the early hours. The Hong Kong Tourism Board stocks two free monthly magazines, *Citylife* and *Where*, which give nightlife and restaurant listings as well as a run-down

Musicians in action

on what's showing at theatres and cinemas. Otherwise you can simply wander through the maze of neon signs and take your pick. For slightly more objective reviews of bars, restaurants and shows study the City section of the *South China Morning Post*, the weekly *HK Magazine* or *BC Magazine* which comes out every two weeks. These last two are handed out free in many bars, restaurants and bookshops. There's always a varied programme of events, ranging from world-class concerts to local amateur dramatic productions.

A highlight of the arts calendar is the annual **Hong Kong Arts Festival**, a three-week dose of international culture in February, with concerts, recitals, plays, jazz, Chinese opera, and innovative productions put on by leading talent from both East and West. Tickets for the shows must be reserved well in advance.

There are more than 30 cinemas in Hong Kong, and the latest Western releases are

The Hong Kong Ballet

shown in some of the larger ones. English-language films have Chinese subtitles. Films with Mandarin dialogue also have Chinese subtitles, for the benefit of Cantonese speakers, and sometimes subtitles in English. The **Hong Kong International Film Festival** takes place in March/April. More than 200 films from all over the world are shown at this two-week event.

The Performing Arts

Performance venues. The theatres in the **Hong Kong Cultural Centre** in Tsim Sha Tsui are the main venues for concerts and opera. Other performing arts centres are the **City Hall** cultural complex, with exhibition halls and theatres that present concerts, plays and films; the **Hong Kong Academy for**

Performing Arts with two major theatres for dance, drama and concert performances; and the **Hong Kong Arts Centre** in Wan Chai, where both local and visiting groups perform. Other centres for concerts, plays and entertainment are Sha Tin Town Hall, Kwai Tsing Theatre in Kwai Chung and the theatres in the Fringe Club for plays and cabaret. Larger arenas, including the Queen Elizabeth Stadium, the Hong Kong Coliseum, and the Ko Shan Theatre in Kowloon play host to various concerts, pop concerts, sporting events and variety shows.

Classical music. The Hong Kong Chinese Orchestra performs new and traditional works; a wide assortment of traditional and Chinese instruments are featured. The Hong Kong Philharmonic Orchestra was founded in 1975. It offers Western classical works and new pieces by Chinese composers in its September-to-June season.

Chinese opera. Cantonese opera is alive and well in Hong Kong, and the two other forms, Beijing and Kunju, are sometimes presented. To most foreigners, this unique art form is likely to be inscrutable at first exposure, but everyone can appreciate the spectacle and the elaborate, glittering costumes. Although the music may seem strange to the unaccustomed ear, it certainly won't send you to sleep with its loud cymbals and drums.

These opera performers have the look of marionettes

Dance. Hong Kong's three professional dance companies – the Hong Kong Ballet Company, the Hong Kong Dance Company and the newer City Contemporary Dance Company – perform regularly, often at the Hong Kong Academy for Performing Arts.

Theatre. The two leading local troupes, the Chung Ying Theatre Company and the Hong Kong Repertory Theatre, perform in Cantonese; there are also English-language performances at the Fringe Club theatres, Lower Albert Road, in Central.

Nightlife

Hong Kong by night can suit any taste – riotous, sedate, raw, or cultured. Sometimes there is a cover charge of HK$50 to HK$200 at clubs, which may or may not include a couple of drinks.

Lan Kwai Fong, just below Hollywood Road, by night

Many of Hong Kong's five-star hotels have bars with live music and some of the best views in the city. The Lobster Bar at the Island Shangri-La is one of the classiest places to listen to live music. The Sky Lounge, on the 18th floor of the Sheraton, and the glitzy Lobby Lounge at the InterContinental, with its floor-to-ceiling harbour views, are great places to take in the Symphony of Lights (8pm), a nightly sound and light display, starring the Hong Kong Island skyline.

The Fringe Club (<www.hkfringe.com.hk>), 21 Lower Albert Road, Central is Hong Kong's best alternative entertainment venue, with jazz, rock and other live music, in addition to an excellent gallery for visual arts and a relaxing rooftop bar.

Pubs are numerous. In Tsim Sha Tsui, Ned Kelly's Last Stand on Ashley Road is an Aussie institution; Delaney's, 71–77 Peking Road, is one of Hong Kong's enduring Irish pubs.

The clubs and bars of **Wan Chai**, long the centre of seedy nightlife, have become almost respectable. Dusk til Dawn, 76–84 Jaffe Road, is a Wan Chai mainstay for all-night partying. Mes Amis at 81–85 Lockhart Road, has a lively dance floor after 11pm at the weekend. A lot of the raunchy action has moved across the harbour to Tsim Sha Tsui East; this is also where you'll find pricey hostess clubs.

The latest trendy area is **SoHo** (South of Hollywood Road), which spreads out around the Central Mid-Levels escalator, to Elgin, Peel and Staunton Streets and Hollywood Road. SoHo, Wyndham Street and the Lan Kwai Fong area have a great choice of restaurants and a lively bar scene. Staunton's at 10–12 Staunton Street, Pickled Pelican on Wyndham Street and Hong Kong Brew House at the top of Lan Kwai Fong are good places to take in the scene and plan your next move.

Causeway Bay is packed with restaurants and bars to visit after late-night shopping. ToTTs in the Excelsior Hotel is a more sophisticated restaurant with music and dancing, while the small bars in the streets around Times Square attract a younger crowd.

Nightlife Tours

Nightlife tours are offered by a number of companies. The most typical of these are harbour cruises, usually including dinner and dancing on board an air-conditioned floating nightclub. There are evening bus tours that include visits to a restaurant and night spots; some tours combine a Chinese banquet with a visit to an open-air market and the panorama from Victoria Peak.

Jogging in the New Territories

SPORTS AND OUTDOOR ACTIVITIES

Beaches. In subtropical Hong Kong you can swim from April to early November. There are more than 40 beaches that are free to the public. Most have lifeguards on duty (Apr–Oct), changing rooms and toilets. On Hong Kong Island, Repulse Bay is the most popular; others are Shek O on the east coast, and Stanley and Deep Water Bay on the south coast. They are very crowded, especially on summer weekends. On the out-lying islands, Cheung Sha is on Lantau, Tung Wan is on Che-ung Chau and Hung Shing Ye and Lo So Shing are on Lamma.

Golf. The Hong Kong Golf Club (tel: 2670 1211) has three 18-hole courses at Fanling in the New Territories. The Discovery Bay Golf Club on Lantau island (tel: 2987 7273) has three nine-hole courses. Both are open to the public on weekdays only. Many Hong Kong residents and visitors cross the border to play at the less expensive world-class courses in Guangdong:

the Guangzhou Luhu Golf and Country Club, <www.luhugolf.com>, or Mission Hills Resort, <www.missionhillsgroup.com>.

Hiking. In the New Territories the famous MacLehose Trail stretches 97km (60 miles) from Sai Kung Peninsula to Tuen Mun. The Lantau Trail is a 69-km (43-mile) circular trail on Lantau Island that begins and ends at Silvermine Bay. Both trails are divided into segments of varying difficulty. Maps of trails are available at the Government Publications Centre, Low Block, Government Offices, 66 Queensway in Central. HKTB also has maps and sponsors the Guided Nature Walks, that include hikes in all the regions of Hong Kong.

Taijiquan (t'ai chi). The HKTB offers free lessons in these exercises that improve concentration and balance, starting at 8am near the Cultural Centre at the Avenue of Stars in Tsim Sha Tsui. Contact the HKTB for more information.

Horseracing. The racing schedule is September to June, and Hong Kong maintains two courses – the older Happy Valley course on Hong Kong Island and the Sha Tin track in the New Territories. The HKTB runs a 'Come Horseracing Tour', which includes entry to the Jockey Club visitors' box and members' enclosure, and a buffet-style meal.

Cricket and rugby. International cricket sixes events are a regular part of the sporting calendar each autumn. The Hong Kong Rugby Sevens has become the world's premier sevens tournament. For one weekend in late March or early April the Hong Kong Stadium hosts international teams and fans who come for the party as much as the sport.

The races at Sha Tin

CHILDREN

Hong Kong has many attractions that appeal to children of all ages. Its many beaches are especially fun for children. Children love riding on Hong Kong's antique trams. A ride on the Peak Tram is sure to provide a thrill, and they'll enjoy the various attractions in the Peak Tower, including Madame Tussauds *(see page 29)*.

Ocean Park *(see page 37)* is very popular with children of all ages, as is Hong Kong Disneyland *(see page 54)*, which opened in 2005 and can be reached aboard the special Disneyland Resort MTR train.

Traditional dance often takes to the streets during festivals

Hong Kong's state-of-the-art interactive museums will appeal to children. The Science Museum in Tsim Sha Tsui East allows children to get their hands on more than half of its 500 exhibits, while the nearby Space Museum has regular screenings on an enormous Omnimax screen in its Space Theatre, making the night sky come vibrantly alive.

For children who love boats, riding the Star Ferry or ferry trips to outlying islands will be exciting, and the Dolphin Watch trip *(see page 113)* is certain to appeal. If you plan to visit during May, the carnival atmosphere of the Cheung Chau Bun Festival, with its high bamboo-and-paper towers covered in steamed buns, will fascinate youngsters.

Calendar of Festivals

For the most up-to-date information, consult the Hong Kong Tourism Board, or pick up a free copy of their *Hong Kong Diary*. Precise dates cannot be given as Chinese festivals are fixed according to the lunar calendar.

January/February: *Lunar New Year* (Spring Festival). Everything in Hong Kong, even businesses, shuts down for three days. It is a time when Chinese families traditionally get together and, though the city seems quieter because so many people leave town or are gathering in their homes, the New Year decorations and lights are fantastic. For most people it means an opportunity to clear out the old – houses are spring-cleaned, people have their hair cut, buy new clothes and settle their debts. The occasion is marked with packed flower shows – the biggest one is in Victoria Park. People visit temples and hand out *lai see* (lucky money) packets to children and unmarried friends, accompanied by the words *Kung hei fat choy* (May you prosper in the New Year). There is a parade on the waterfront, and an elaborate fireworks display lights up the harbour. With factories and businesses closed for at least a week on the mainland, travelling to China is best avoided.

February: *Spring Lantern Festival (Yuen Siu)*. The last day of the Chinese New Year celebrations is also known as Chinese Valentine's Day, since it was traditionally the time when unmarried women donned their finest clothes and ventured out with their chaperones to meet some eligible young men.

April: *Ching Ming Festival*. This Confucian festival, timed to the solar calendar, is one of two annual holidays on which to honour the dead. Ancestors' graves are swept and offerings of food, wine or flowers are made, while gold and silver 'money' is burned to give the ancestors enough to spend in the afterworld.

April/May: *Birthday of Tin Hau*. The Taoist Goddess of the Sea is honoured by fishing communities with prayers for safe voyages and good catches. The liveliest celebration is at Joss House Bay, where decorated junks and sampans converge with offerings. Spectators can reach the beach by special excursion boats. Smaller-scale celebrations, including lion-dancing, take place at other Tin Hau temples, notably at Aberdeen.

May: *Birthday of the Lord Buddha.* In Buddhist temples throughout the territory, the Buddha's image is bathed in scented water to symbolise the washing away of sins. *Cheung Chau Bun Festival.* This ritual was apparently initiated when human bones were discovered during construction of the Pak Tai Temple. Fearing that the temple would be haunted by the spirits which had been disturbed, the island's inhabitants sought to appease them by putting out offerings of steamed buns. Today, the event is celebrated by the erection of three 16-m (52-ft) bamboo towers, each piled with some 5,000 pink and white lotus-paste buns. The festival lasts for about eight or nine days; processions, lion and dragon dances and traditional rites at the temple give the island a carnival atmosphere.

May/June: *Dragon Boat Festival (Tuen Ng).* Oarsmen in long, thin dragon boats race to the beat of big bass drums and Chinese gongs. Annual International Dragon Boat races are usually held a few days after the festival in June or July.

July: *Birthday of Lu Pan.* The Taoist patron saint of carpenters and builders is honoured with celebratory banquets.

August: *Seven Sisters' (Maidens') Festival.* A festival for lovers, based on an old legend. Women praying for husbands leave offerings at Lovers' Rock. *Hungry Ghosts Festival (Yue Lan).* Paper offerings are burned and food left out to placate ghosts temporarily released from the underworld.

September: *Mid-Autumn Festival.* Celebrating the year's harvest, this one is a children's favourite. As the full moon rises, tots carrying paper lanterns of traditional or space-age design congregate in open spaces or high places to admire the poetic sight. They eat moon cakes (ground sesame and lotus seeds or dates, perhaps enriched with duck egg) and take full advantage of being allowed to stay up late.

October: *Cheung Yeung Festival.* Nineteen centuries ago, so it is said, a man visited the hills on the advice of a fortune-teller. When he returned he found he was the sole survivor of a calamity. On the ninth day of the ninth moon, people visit the hillside graves of their ancestors and try to reach some high place for luck.

EATING OUT

The Chinese care about food with a passion only the French can rival. For the Chinese, eating is a pleasure imbued with philosophical profundities: even the dead are offered food and wine to make their journey from this life more peaceful.

Chinese restaurants are a place for family and social gatherings. Eating out is one of the main forms of socialising, and the Chinese usually eat in large groups. The food is best enjoyed if there is a variety of dishes. If Chinese hosts invite you to a restaurant, put yourself in their hands; they will try to order according to their impression of your tastes.

Rice to meet you

A common Cantonese greeting is 'Lay sik jaw fan may ah?' – ('Have you had your rice yet?')

Chefs have a demanding clientele. Chinese gourmets demand the freshest food from local farms and the sea – they require not only the best flavours but colour, texture and presentation to enhance the pleasure of the food. A proper Chinese meal is orchestrated, and must contain a harmonious progression from sweet to sour, crunchy to tender. A Chinese banquet is a triumph of the well-rounded art of food.

You rarely find a bad Chinese meal here. The big problem is how to choose from among the thousands of restaurants, and then among the hundreds of items on the menu. Let the waiter help you to choose just the right amount of food with the best range of tastes and textures.

In Hong Kong you'll find restaurants offering cuisines from all over Asia, and a wide choice of Western cuisines, especially French but also Italian, Dutch, and Mexican, as well as steak, pizza and kosher food. Vegetarians do not have an easy time in Hong Kong. Most Chinese chefs use chicken or other meat stock routinely in otherwise vegetarian dishes, but there are a handful devoted to a purely vegetarian cuisine.

Meal Times

Most hotels serve a breakfast buffet of Chinese and Western food from about 7 to 10am. At lunchtime business people pack the restaurants from 1 to 2.30pm. Dinner is between 7.30 and 9.30pm, but Chinese restaurants are flexible; many are open from early in the morning until midnight without a break.

A traditional Chinese breakfast consists of *congee*, a rice gruel or porridge to which almost anything may be added. At back-street breakfast stalls you'll also see the early risers digging into noodle soup with chunks of vegetable or pork.

A breakfast chef at the Harbour Plaza Hotel

Regional Cuisines

Chinese food comes in half a dozen principal styles, all very different from one another. In Hong Kong every major school of Chinese cooking is represented; restaurants have inherited recipes and brilliant cooks from all parts of China.

Cantonese

For visitors, this is probably the most familiar Chinese cuisine, as so many Cantonese emigrated, opened restaurants, and introduced new tastes to diners in the West. Cantonese food is either

Colourful Cantonese cuisine

steamed or stir-fried, cooking methods that capture the flavour of the ingredients as well as the colour and vita-mins. A vast range of ingre-dients is used, and the flavours are many and often delicately understated.

Garoupa, a delicious local fish, comes steamed with ginger, spring onions and soy sauce, with a touch of garlic. Prawns come in a sauce of sugar, vinegar, soy and ket-chup, coloured with the ad-dition of crisp red and green peppers and pineapple chunks. Lemon chicken consists of fried chunks of tender chicken in a creamy sauce of sugared lemon juice and chicken broth. A hearty soup is crabmeat and corn soup; soup is usually served towards the end of the meal. Steamed white rice is normally served with a Can-tonese meal.

Chiu Chow

This regional cuisine from the Swatow region of southeast China excels in novel seasonings and rich sauces. Chefs also pride themselves on their amazing vegetable carvings that are part of every Chiu Chow banquet. Before and after dinner you will be presented with tiny cups of a strong and bitter tea, known as Iron Buddha.

Two very expensive Chiu Chow delicacies are shark's fin and bird's nest. (Note that sharks have become endan-gered because of over-fishing and eating shark's fin is high-ly wasteful as the fin is the only part of the animal that is eaten.) A typical dish is minced pigeon: the pigeon meat is minced and fried with herbs, and eaten wrapped in lettuce leaves. In Chiu Chow restaurants *congee* is often served instead of rice.

Beijing (Peking)

The Chinese emperors made Beijing the gourmet centre of the country, and Hong Kong's Peking restaurants still present truly imperial banquets (ordered in advance) with everything from nuts to soup, in that order. Northern food tends to be richer than Cantonese food. Don't miss the dramatic smashing of the clay around 'beggar's chicken', or one of the world's most delicious eating experiences, Peking duck. The duck is honey-coated before roasting and is cut at the table. The celebrants put chunks of the crisp skin along with spring onions and a sweet

Chinese dining offers a wide variety of experiences, from humble street food to gourmet cuisine with a view

Roasted duck is a common sight at market stalls

sauce, onto delicate pancakes, which are then rolled up and devoured. The meat is then taken away to be stir fried with other ingredients and served as a separate dish.

Wheat, not rice, is the staple food in northern China. Peking restaurants serve noodles and various kinds of bread. They also specialise in wonderful dumplings, stuffed with meat or vegetables.

Shanghai

Shanghai restaurants also serve a dish known as 'beggar's chicken'. According to legend, the inventor was a tramp who stole a chicken but had no way to cook it. After tossing in some salt and onion, he covered the entire bird in a shell of mud, then roasted it on a fire. When the mud was baked dry and he smashed the coating – the feathers came off with the clay and all the juicy tenderness of the bird remained. The recipe has become more sophisticated as mushrooms, pickled cabbage, shredded pork, bamboo shoots and wine are added to the stuffing.

Shanghai food is an amalgam of a number of Chinese cuisines from surrounding cities. It tends to be more diverse and complicated as well as more thoroughly cooked than, say, Cantonese. Chili peppers, garlic, and ginger are used in moderation. Freshwater hairy crab, imported from Shanghai in autumn, steamed and eaten with the hands, is a popular dish as is *xiao long bao*, a Chinese-style bun filled with a mixture of minced pork, ginger, spring onion and sesame oil. Shanghai diners usually prefer noodles to rice.

Sichuan

This food from southwestern China has become popular in America. It produces such sharp, hot flavours that it first takes your breath away, then awakens your palate. Once the fiery shock of the garlic-enhanced peppers has subsided, you can distinguish the other many elements in unlikely coexistence – bitter, sweet, fruity, tart and sour.

Smoked duck, Sichuan style, is marinated in rice wine, with ginger and an array of spices, then steamed before being smoked over a specially composed wood fire. Equally delicious is deep-fried beef with vegetables, a dish in which the meat and most of the other ingredients – carrots, celery, peppers, garlic – are shredded and slowly fried over a low flame.

All Chinese foods are pleasing to the eye, but there are some Sichuan foods that appeal to the ear. 'Thunder' dishes are topped with crisp rice, which sizzles and pops on contact with the other ingredients.

Try Chopsticks

You'll lose face – and fun – if you don't learn to use chopsticks to eat your food in Hong Kong. There's no reason to feel self-conscious – the Chinese are tolerant when it comes to table manners.

Begin by settling the bottom stick firmly at the conjunction of the thumb and forefinger, balancing it against the first joint of the ring finger. The second stick pivots around the fulcrum made by the tip of the thumb and the inside of the forefinger.

Remember not to lay your chopsticks across each other, and never place them across the rice bowl, but rest them on the holder provided or against a plate.

Forks and knives are supplied in most restaurants. If it's any consolation, many Chinese don't feel quite at home with them either.

Hakka

The name Hakka means 'guest people', referring to their migration to this region from northern China many centuries ago. Hakka cuisine involves the use of simple ingredients, especially versatile bean curd. Look for an ingenious dish called salted chicken; a coating of salt contains and increases the flavours while the bird is being baked.

Dim Sum

Late breakfast or lunch can consist of tea and *dim sum*, the small snacks which add up to a delicious, filling meal. Servers wander from table to table chanting the Cantonese names of the foods contained in bamboo steamers on their trays or carts. Choose whatever looks interesting – from spring rolls to spare ribs and dozens of different dumpling varieties, including: *siu mai* (pork and shrimp dumplings), *har gau* (delicate steam-

Dim Sum includes dozens of different dumpling varieties

ed shrimp dumplings), and *cha siu bau* (barbecued pork buns). When you ask for the bill, the waiter will count the number of empty dishes on the table and tot up the bill.

Drinks

The Chinese having a dinner party at the table next to you are probably drinking Cognac with their meal. Hong Kong claims the world's highest per capita consumption of brandy, possibly because of a vague belief that it has aphrodisiac qualities. European and Australian table wines are also available, and they are now relatively inexpensive.

Few visitors develop a taste for Chinese wines, despite their 4,000-year history. Some are too sweet, others too strong. Unlike the Chinese grape and rice wines, the wheat-based wines are notorious for their alcoholic power. Mao Tai is a breathtaking case in point.

The best choice for the visitor is beer. The locally brewed San Miguel is cheap and refreshing. Tsingtao beer from China has a hearty European taste. You'll also find a large selection of European brands, some of them brewed locally under licence.

The Chinese have been drinking tea for many centuries as a thirst-quencher, general reviver, and ceremonial beverage. Tea in China is drunk without sugar or milk, although 'English-style' tea is available. It's worth making the effort to learn to appreciate the many varieties of tea and their histories. For a caffeine-free alternative, ask for hot chrysanthemum tea, brewed from the dried petals of the flower.

Rounding off the beverage list are familiar soft drinks and tasty tropical fruit juices. Coffee can be enjoyed throughout the city at chains like Starbucks, Pacific Coffee and Delifrance.

To Help You Order...

Waiter!/Waitress!	**Mgoi!**
Have you a table?	**Yau mo toi ah?**
Do you have a set menu?	**Yau mo to chaan a?**
I'd like a/an/some...	**Ngor seung yiu...**
The bill, please.	**Mai dan, m goi.**

beer	**bei jau**	ice	**bing**
beef	**ngau yuk**	lamb	**yurng yuk**
cake	**daan go**	menu	**chan pye**
chicken	**gai**	pork	**ju-ee yuk**
chopsticks	**fai ji**	rice	**faan**
cup	**bui**	steak	**ngau pa**
dessert	**tim bun**	soup	**tong**
fish	**yue**	tea	**cha**
fruit	**sang gwo**	water	**sui**
glass	**bor lay bui**	wine	**jau**

...and Read the Menu

蟹肉豆腐羹	bean curd and crabmeat soup
麻婆豆腐	bean curd with pork in pepper sauce
合桃鷄丁	diced chicken with walnuts
腰果肉丁	diced pork with cashew nuts
干燒冬筍	fried bamboo shoots and cabbage
炒蟮糊	fried eel with soya sauce
清炒蝦仁	fried shrimps
青椒肉絲	fried sliced pork with green pepper
菜扒鮮菇	mushrooms with vegetables
辣子鷄丁	shredded chicken with green pepper
豉椒牛肉	sliced beef with green pepper and bean sauce
三絲湯	sliced chicken, abalone and prawn soup
紅燒魚片	sliced fish with brown sauce
糟溜黃魚	stewed yellow fish
咕嚕肉	sweet and sour pork
鷄油津白	Tientsin cabbage and asparagus

HANDY TRAVEL TIPS

An A–Z Summary of Practical Information

A

ACCOMMODATION (see also the list of RECOMMENDED HOTELS on page 128)

Most of Hong Kong's 50,000 hotel rooms are in luxury or first-class hotels, so finding moderately-priced or budget accommodation is not always easy. Hong Kong's high seasons are October to early December, and March and April. In other months, particularly in summer, prices may drop, and bonuses such as upgrades, free airport transport and discounts may be offered.

The price of a room in Hong Kong often depends upon its view. For the best rates, check with a travel agent or look for a package that offers hotel and airfare. Rooms tend to be small except in the most expensive places. High- and mid-range hotels are all members of the Hong Kong Hotel Association (HKHA; <www.hkha.org>); check for membership in this organisation when booking an inexpensive accommodation.

Advance reservations are essential for moderately-priced hotels, and advisable for all others. For visitors arriving by air without reservations, there are two HKHA desks in arrivals which can arrange a room with any hotel associated with it. The service is provided free of charge and the desk is open from 6am–1am.

Hong Kong hotels include all the major international chains. Many of the more modest establishments offer services comparable to first-class hotels. Posted rates cover the room price only; a 10 percent service charge and a 3 percent government tax are added to the bill at check-out time.

AIRPORT

Arriving. International flights land at Hong Kong International Airport at Chek Lap Kok on Lantau Island, <www.hkairport.com>. Immigration and customs checks are efficient in this modern airport. Beyond the baggage inspection area you will find a bank, money changers, HKHA counters and two HKTB desks for tourist information. The Ground Transportation Centre is the place to go for information about transportation into the city, or for taxis and limousine service.

Airport Express (AEL). (tel: 2881 8888) This rail link is the quickest and most efficient way to get into the city. Trains run every 12 minutes from 5.54am–12.48am daily to Kowloon (20 minutes) and Hong Kong station in Central (23 minutes). Buy tickets from the automatic machines.

Airbuses. (tel: 2873 0818) The buses serve all major hotels. Take A21 to Kowloon, A11 and A12 to Hong Kong Island. Travel time is about an hour. Buy tickets at the Commercial Service Counter or have exact fare ready.

Limousines and taxis. Major hotels operate their own limousine services; go to the HKHA desk, or look for the hotel pick-up counters. If you take a taxi, you should be charged only what the meter reads, plus tolls and a charge for each piece of luggage placed in the boot.

Departure. Most major airlines, including Cathay Pacific, United and Singapore Airlines, allow you to check in for your return flight at either Hong Kong Central Station or Kowloon Station up to 24 hours before your departure. Boarding passes will be issued, and luggage transferred to the airport.

B

BUDGETING FOR YOUR TRIP

To give you an idea of what to expect in terms of cost, here are some average prices in Hong Kong dollars. However, remember that prices change, so they should be regarded as approximate.

Airport transfer. Limousine from the airport to your hotel, about HK$500; taxis HK$250–400, plus tolls and luggage; Airport Express HK$90–100; Airbus HK$33–45.

Buses and trams. Buses HK$1.20–45, trams HK$2 for adults, HK$1 for children, minibuses and maxicabs HK$2–22.50, Peak Tram HK$20 (one way), HK$30 (return) for adults, HK$6 (one way), HK$9 (return) for children.

Car rental. A compact car costs around HK$750 a day. A car or limo with a driver costs around HK$160 an hour.

Ferries. Star Ferry HK$2.20; island ferries HK$10–31; Macau ferry HK$141–275.

Hotels. Luxury hotels range upwards from HK$2,500, top hotels from HK$1,800; medium range hotels begin at around HK$950, and inexpensive hotels less than HK$950. All add 10 percent service charge and 3 percent government tax to the bill.

MTR. Mass Transit Railway fares range from HK$4 up to HK$26, depending on distance.

Meals and drinks. In a moderately-priced restaurant: set lunch HK$80–150, dinner HK$150–350; buffets are generally good value for money.

Taxis. HK$15 for the first 2km (1.2 miles), HK$1.40 for each succeeding 200m, HK$20 for journeys via Cross Harbour Tunnel or HK$30 via the Eastern Harbour Crossing (to cover driver's return toll), and HK$5 for each piece of baggage.

Trains. From Kowloon to Lo Wu on the border with mainland China, first class HK$66, standard class HK$33.

C

CAR HIRE (See also DRIVING)

Driving in Hong Kong is not recommended. Traffic can be a nightmare, streets are narrow and crowded, and parking often nearly impossible. Hong Kong's public transport system is so well organised that driving is never as quick and convenient as the MTR or a bus. Moreover, distances are short, and walking is often an easy option.

All international and many local car hire firms operate in Hong Kong offering both self-drive and chauffeur-driven cars. Japanese, European and American models are available.

Major credit cards are accepted. To hire a car, drivers must be over 25 years old and have held a valid licence from their home country or an international licence for two years.

CLIMATE

The best time to visit Hong Kong is in October or November, when the temperature and humidity drop and days are clear and sunny. From December until late February you'll find the air moderately cool with the humidity still low (around 73 percent). In spring the humidity and temperature start rising. March and April can be very pleasant, but from May to mid-September it's extremely hot and often wet, with most of the annual rainfall recorded during these months.

The following chart gives an idea of the average monthly temperatures in Hong Kong, and the number of rainy days per month.

	J	F	M	A	M	J	J	A	S	O	N	D
°C	15	15	18	22	25	28	28	28	27	25	21	17
°F	59	59	64	72	77	82	82	82	81	77	70	63
Days of Rain	6	8	11	12	16	21	19	17	14	8	6	5

CLOTHING

From May to September lightweight summer clothing is called for, and a raincoat and umbrella might come in handy. In restaurants and hotels, beware of the air-conditioning, which can reduce the temperature substantially. From late September to early December shirtsleeves and sweaters are appropriate, while in winter – late December to February – a wool suit and a warm jacket or light coat are advisable.

Informality is generally the rule in dress. For sightseeing and shopping, virtually any fashion is appropriate. Shorts and T-shirts are perfectly acceptable, but shorts and halter tops are out of place at the more upmarket restaurants and in Chinese temples. You'll see people in formal business attire in Hong Kong's Central business district. Bring along comfortable shoes for the steep slopes of Hong Kong.

CONSULATES

Consulates are generally open Monday–Friday, 9am–noon and 2–4 or 5pm. Various sections may be open at different hours; to make sure, telephone first.

Australia: 23rd–24th floors, Harbour Centre, 25 Harbour Road, Wan Chai, tel: 2827 8881.

Canada: 12th–14th floors, Tower 1, Exchange Square, 8 Connaught Place, Central, tel: 2810 4321.

New Zealand: 65th floor, Central Plaza, 18 Harbour Road, Wan Chai, tel: 2877 4488.

UK: 1 Supreme Court Road, Central, tel: 2901 3000.

US: 26 Garden Road, Central, tel: 2523 9011.

CRIME AND SAFETY (See also EMERGENCIES and POLICE)

Hong Kong is a safe city, night and day. The streets are usually full of people until late at night. Signs everywhere warn you to 'beware of pickpockets'. This particularly applies to crowded areas, and Hong Kong has some of the most crowded places you've ever seen. Be especially careful in crowded markets such as the Temple Street Night Market, and on rush-hour buses and MTR trains. It is best to leave your valuables in a hotel safe.

CUSTOMS AND ENTRY REQUIREMENTS

For most nationalities, only a passport is required for entry into Hong Kong. Subjects of the UK can stay up to six months without a visa; Canadians, Australians and New Zealanders and US citizens can stay for three months. To enter Macau, only a passport is needed, and most visitors can stay up to 20 days without a visa.

Visas are required for entry into the People's Republic of China, so if you are visiting Guangzhou, Shenzhen, or taking any other excursion over the border, you will need a visa. Short-term tours to China may include visas; otherwise visas can be arranged at the office of China Travel Service (CITS), 27–33 Nathan Road, Tsim Sha Tsui.

You can bring into Hong Kong duty-free: 200 cigarettes or 50 cigars or 250 grams tobacco, and 1 litre spirits or 1 litre wine. Firearms are strictly controlled, and can only be brought in by special permit. There are no currency restrictions.

When returning home, duty-free quotas are as follows. Australia: A\$400 worth of merchandise, 250 cigarettes or 250 grams tobacco and 1 litre spirits or 1 litre wine. Canada: Can\$500 worth of merchandise, 200 cigarettes, 400 grams tobacco, 50 cigars, 1.4 litres spirits and 1.4 litre wine. New Zealand: NZ\$700 worth of merchandise, 200 cigarettes or 50 cigars or 250 grams tobacco and 1.1 litres spirits and 4.5 litres wine. UK: £145 worth of merchandise, 200 cigarettes or 50 cigars or 250 grams tobacco and 1 litre spirits and 2 litres wine. US: US\$400 worth of merchandise, 200 cigarettes and 100 cigars, 1 litre wine or spirits; Cuban cigars, plants or fresh foodstuffs are prohibited; antiques over 100 years old are duty-free.

D

DRIVING (See also CAR RENTAL)

Anyone over 18 with a valid licence and third-party insurance can drive in Hong Kong for 12 months without having to pay for a local licence. Drivers must carry a valid driver's licence and photo identification at all times.

Road conditions. Congestion is a serious problem in the city, sometimes leading to impatient driving. Beware of inattentive pedestrians. Good highways connect to the New Territories and the airport.

Rules and regulations. As in Britain and Australia, Hong Kong traffic keeps to the left. All passengers in private cars, front and back, are required to wear seatbelts. Drivers may not use hand-held mobile phones while driving. Note that across the border in China, as in Europe and the US, cars keep to the right. The speed limit is 30mph (50km/h) in towns, elsewhere as marked.

Parking. This can be a headache, especially in the central areas, despite the multi-storey car parks. In busy streets, meters operate from 8am to midnight Monday–Saturday, and wardens are ever alert.

Breakdowns. Telephone the agency from which you hired the car. In an emergency, dial 999 for the police. The Automobile Association is at 391 Nathan Road, Yau Ma Tei, tel: 2739 5273.

Road signs. Most road signs in Hong Kong are the standard international pictographs.

The following words may help you in explaining your problems to non-English-speaking Chinese:

There's been an accident.	Yow yee oy.
collision	jong che
flat tire	bow tai
Help!	Gau meng ah!
Police!	Geng tsa!

E

ELECTRICITY

Standard voltage in Hong Kong is 220-volt, 50-cycle AC. Many hotels have razor fittings for all standard plugs and voltages. For other units, transformers and plug adapters will be needed; you may need a plug for your laptop even if it is equipped to deal with both 220 and 110 volts. Most hotels supply hairdryers.

EMERGENCIES

Dial 999 for Police, Fire, or Ambulance departments. St John's Ambulance Brigade is a free service, tel: 2576 6555 on Hong Kong island, 2713 5555 in Kowloon, or 2639 2555 in the New Territories. Hospitals with 24-hour emergency services are: Queen Mary Hospital, 102 Pokfulam Road, Hong Kong Island, tel: 2855 3838; Queen Elizabeth Hospital, 30 Gascoigne Road, Kowloon, tel: 2958 8888; and Hong Kong Adventist Hospital, 40 Stubbs Road, Hong Kong Island, tel: 2574 6211. Many hotels have doctors on call.

In Macau, dial 999 in an emergency, or tel: 2857 3333 for the police and tel: 2857 2222 for fire.

G

GAY AND LESBIAN TRAVELLERS

Hong Kong is still fairly conservative, despite a softening of anti-gay attitudes since the 1991 Crimes Ordinance that de-criminalised homosexual acts. There's a gay scene around Glenealy and Wyndham Street in Central. For gay nightlife information look out for free publication *G Magazine* or visit <www.gaystation.com.hk>.

GETTING THERE

From North America. Several airlines offer direct flights between North American cities and Hong Kong. Hong Kong's Cathay Pacific Airways (tel: 1-800/233-2742; <www.cathaypacific.com>) has daily flights from Los Angeles, San Francisco, New York, Vancouver and Toronto. Air Canada (tel: 1-888/247 2262; <www.aircanada.ca>) has daily flights from Vancouver and five services per week from Toronto; Continental Airlines (tel: 1-800/231 0856; <www.continental.com>) has daily flights from Newark, NJ; Singapore Airlines (tel: 1-800/742-3333; <www.singaporeair.com>) has daily flights from San Francisco; and United Airlines (tel: 1-800/241 6522; <www.united.com>) has daily services from San Francisco and Chicago.

Other airlines with direct flights from North America include Northwest Airlines (tel: 800/225-2525; <www.nwa.com>), which also flies to Macau; Japan Airlines (tel: 800/525-3663; <www.japan air.com>); Korean Air (tel: 800/438-5000; <www.koreanair.com>). China Airlines (tel: 800/227-5118; <www.china-airlines.com>) flies daily from New York with a change in Taipei.

From the UK. CathayPacific (tel: 020/8834 8888), British Airways (tel: 0870/8509 850; <www.britishairways.com>), and Virgin Atlantic Airways (tel: 0870/380 2007; <www.virgin-atlantic.com>) offer daily nonstop services from London to Hong Kong.

From Australia and New Zealand. Both Qantas (tel: 131313; <www.qantas.com.au>) and Cathay Pacific (tel: 131747) offer daily nonstop services from Sydney and Melbourne. From New Zealand, Cathay Pacific (tel: 0800/800 454) flies daily from Auckland.

GUIDES AND TOURS

There are all kinds of organised tours in Hong Kong, from orientation tours of the city, night cruises of the harbour, and tours of the islands to trips farther afield to Macau, Shenzhen and Guangzhou.

The Hong Kong Tourism Board (HKTB) organises a large assortment of tours. Something well worth considering is the HKTB's series of free so-called 'Cultural Kaleidoscope Tours'. They include a ride in Hong Kong's last genuine sailing junk, classes in tai chi, pearl and jade shopping, feng shui, lessons in Cantonese opera appreciation and tea drinking as well as a kung fu corner. They are only open to bona fide tourists. Book a place with the HKTB.

Tour operators include Gray Line Tours of Hong Kong Ltd., 5/F 72 Nathan Road, Tsim Sha Tsui (tel: 2368 7111); Watertours, at Shop 5C, Ground Floor, Star House, Tsim Sha Tsui (tel: 2926 3868), is the largest operator of boat and junk cruises; Splendid Tours and Travel Ltd (tel: 2316 2151) has night cruises among its offerings; and China Travel Service of Hong Kong Ltd (CITS) runs 1–3-day tours of Guangzhou and other South China destinations.

Most interesting for the visitor who has a few days in Hong Kong are the theme tours sponsored by HKTB. Outstanding is the 'Heritage Tour', which takes you to historic sites in the New Territories. 'The Land Between Tour' takes you to traditional villages in the New Territories. The 'Feng Shui Tour' explores this traditional concept *(see box, page 24).*

Hong Kong Dolphinwatch Ltd., 1528 Star House, Tsim Sha Tsui (tel: 2984 1414; <www.hkdolphinwatch.com>) has a half-day eco-cruise to sight Hong Kong's threatened pink dolphins.

If you are interested in hiring a guide for a group or a personal guide, contact HKTB in Hong Kong. Contact CITS for guides in other South China destinations.

H

HEALTH AND MEDICAL CARE *(See also EMERGENCIES)*

There are no special health precautions to take in Hong Kong. No vaccinations are needed. Food is safe, even in roadside stalls, and you can safely drink the water, though most people prefer bottled water. Avoid eating locally caught shellfish and oysters, and never eat them raw; most restaurants use imported or farmed varieties. Be aware that outside major hotels, MSG (monosodium glutamate) is widely used.

Travelling into China requires a few extra precautions. You should not drink the tap water; drink only bottled water and use bottled water to brush your teeth. However, the thermos of hot water supplied in all hotel rooms is perfectly safe to drink. It is also wise not to eat raw food in China; choose fruit that can be peeled.

a bottle of drinking water	yat tchun sui
I want to see a...	Ngor yiu tai...
doctor	yee sang
dentist	nga yee

During the hot, humid summer months, remember to limit exposure to the sun. Wear a hat and use a sunscreen. Always carry a bottle of water, especially when hiking.

HOLIDAYS

Thanks to the convergence of British and Chinese traditions, Hong Kong celebrates 17 holidays a year. Though the banks close, most businesses carry on as usual. The only holiday on which Hong Kong really shuts down is the Lunar New Year. Chinese holidays are fixed according to the lunar calendar, so exact dates cannot always be given.

January 1	New Year's Day
January or February	Lunar New Year (3 days)
March or April	Easter (Good Friday, Easter Monday)
April	Ching Ming Festival
May 1	Labour Day
May	Buddha's Birthday
May or June	Tuen Ng (Dragon Boat) Festival
July 1 (or first weekday)	Establishment Day of the Special Administrative Region
September	The day following the mid-Autumn Festival
October 1	National Day
October	Chung Yeung Festival
December 25	Christmas Day
December 26	Boxing Day (day after Christmas)

L

LANGUAGE

The official languages of Hong Kong are English and Chinese. While Chinese can be called the world's most widely spoken language, it actually has innumerable dialects – people from Beijing can't understand a word that people from Hong Kong say; in fact they can't even understand what people from Shanghai say. What has bound the country together over thousands of years is the written language.

Each Chinese character represents an idea – a meaning, not a sound. There are about 50,000 characters; some 5,000 of these are in common use. Writing a single character may require from 1 to 33 strokes. Written Chinese is a subtle language – choice of one character over another can convey delicate shades of meaning. Handwriting style is also important – the Chinese consider calligraphy a serious art form. Chinese is traditionally written in columns, read from top to bottom and right to left. However, today you often see printed Chinese characters presented much like a European language.

Putonghua, or Mandarin, is China's official language and is gradually becoming the lingua franca all over mainland China. Cantonese is spoken in Hong Kong and South China. While Putonghua has only four tones, Cantonese uses up to nine different tonal inflections to distinguish otherwise identical syllables. This makes Cantonese an especially difficult language for foreigners to learn.

The following approximations of Cantonese greetings may help you make contact with the locals:

Good morning	Jo sahn
Good afternoon	Ng on
Good evening	Mang on
Good night	Jo tow
Goodbye	Joy geen
Please (for service)	M goi
Please (invitation)	Ching
Thank you (for service)	M goi
Thank you (for a gift)	Daw jeh

Here are some everyday Hong Kong words:

amah	housemaid
chop	seal or stamp on a document
fung shui	lucky siting of building or graves
gwailo	Europeans, foreigners
hong	big business firm
joss	luck
yam seng	'cheers', 'bottoms up'

Getting around is difficult when place names are pronounced differently in English and Cantonese. Kowloon (Nine Dragons) sounds similar in both languages; here are some that differ:

Aberdeen	**Heung Gong Jai**
Causeway Bay	**Tung Lo Wan**
Central District	**Jung Wan**
Cross Harbour Tunnel	**Hoi Dai Sui Do**
Happy Valley	**Pau Ma Dei**
Ocean Park	**Hoi Yeung Gung Yuen**
The Peak	**San Deng**
Peak Tram	**Lam Che**
Repulse Bay	**Chin Sui Wan**
Stanley	**Chek Chue**
Star Ferry Pier	**Tin Sing Ma Tau**

MEDIA

Newspapers and magazines. Local English-language dailies are the *South China Morning Post* and *The Standard*; the *China Daily* is a Hong Kong-published version of China's national English-language daily. The *Asian Wall Street Journal,* published Monday–Friday in Hong Kong, focuses on business and financial affairs. The *International Herald Tribune,* edited in Paris, is printed simultaneously in Hong Kong six days a week. Newspapers and magazines from Europe, Asia and the US are easily available at hotels and bookshops.

Radio and television. Hong Kong has two free-to-air TV channels in English as well as two in Chinese. The Chinese channels sometimes show foreign-language films which are dubbed into Cantonese; satellite and cable stations are also available. All hotels provide a selection of international news and entertainment television channels.

There are six English-language radio channels providing a broad range, from easy listening to news and current affairs. The BBC World Service also broadcasts 24 hours a day at 675 kHz.

MONEY

Currency. Hong Kong's currency is freely convertible, and is pegged to the US dollar at a rate of around 7.8. The Hong Kong dollar is divided into 100 cents. Banknotes are circulated in denominations of HK$10, HK$20, HK$50, HK$100, HK$500 and HK$1,000. Banknotes are issued by three local banks, Hongkong and Shanghai Banking Corporation, the Bank of China and the Standard Chartered Bank. Coins, however, are minted by the Hong Kong government; they come in denominations of 10, 20 and 50 cents and HK$1, HK$2, HK$5 and HK$10. Britain's Queen Elizabeth, who once appeared on these coins, has been replaced by the flower of the bauhinia tree, Hong Kong's regional emblem.

Currency in Macau and China. In China, the *renminbi* (RMB) or *yuan* is not a fully convertible currency; you can change your Hong Kong dollars (or any other currency) to *yuan* in China but you are only allowed to change *yuan* back to foreign currency provided you have a receipt of the original transaction. However, Hong Kong dollars are accepted in both Guangzhou and Shenzhen. Macau's currency is the *pataca*, and the same rules apply. Both the *yuan* and the *pataca* have an exchange value roughly the equivalent of the Hong Kong dollar, i.e. you will be charged in Hong Kong dollars about what you would be charged if you were paying in *patacas* or *yuan*.

Currency exchange. Foreign currencies can be exchanged at banks, hotels, money changers and major shopping outlets. Banks have better exchange rates, but charge a commission. Licensed money changers charge no commission, but the rates offered are about equivalent to a 5 percent commission. Money changers are found in all tourist areas and are open on holidays and late into the evening.

ATMs. ATMs are found all over Hong Kong, and banks do not usually charge a fee for the service. There are ATMs in Guangzhou and Shenzhen, but these are harder to find.

Credit cards. Credit cards and charge cards are accepted everywhere you go in Hong Kong. Major hotels, restaurants and shops in China also accept the well-known credit cards.

Traveller's cheques. Traveller's cheques are widely accepted in shops, though you'll probably get a better exchange rate at a bank. You must show your passport when you cash a cheque. They are particularly useful in China, where you may not find an ATM.

OPENING HOURS

Most government offices are open 9am–1pm and 2–5pm Monday–Friday, and 9am–1pm Saturday.

Banking hours are usually 9am–4.30pm Monday–Friday, and 9am–12.30pm Saturday. Some banks stop transactions an hour before closing time.

Business offices are normally open Monday–Friday 9am–5pm, closed for lunch 1–2pm; Saturday 9am–5pm. Most post offices are open Monday–Friday 9.30am–5pm and Saturday until 1pm.

Most shops are open seven days a week. Shops on Hong Kong Island are open 10am–7pm in Central, 10am–9.30 pm in Wan Chai, and 10am–10pm or later in Causeway Bay and Tsim Sha Tsui.

Museums are open from 10 or 11am–6pm. Most close one day a week, and some close on public holidays.

P

POLICE

The Hong Kong Police Force is one of the world's best equipped. The police deal not only with crime and traffic but also coast guard duties. Living up to Hong Kong's reputation as a fashion centre, they dress in smart, tailored uniforms. Most police can speak some English.

Where's the police station, please?	Chai goon haih been do a, m goi?

POST OFFICES

The main post office is on Hong Kong Island at 2 Connaught Place, near the Central Airport Express station. There is a philatelic center on the ground floor; mailing and stamps are taken care of on the first floor. In Kowloon, post offices are located at 405 Nathan Road, between the Jordan and Yau Ma Tei underground stations, and at 10 Middle Road, one block north of Salisbury Road. For information, tel: 2921 2222.

Post offices in Hong Kong deal only with mailing letters and packages. For faxing and other services, see the business centre in your hotel.

PUBLIC TRANSPORT

Hong Kong's public transport system is one of the most efficient and easy to use anywhere; it's also remarkably inexpensive. Be aware that buses, ferries, and trams require the exact fare, so it is wise to carry some small change. The Octopus Card, which can be purchased at MTR stations, is a convenient electronic card accepted on most buses and ferries, trams and the MTR system (including the trains in the New Territories and the Airport Express Line). It costs HK$150 (including an HK$50 refundable deposit), and can be reloaded in units of HK$50 or HK$100 at MTR stations or convenience stores.

MTR. Hong Kong's Mass Transit Railway is one of the world's most modern, attractive, and easy-to-use undergrounds. It operates daily 6am–1am, and connects Kowloon, Hong Kong Island, the New Territories and Lantau. The lines (including the dedicated Disneyland Resort line) are colour-coded; signs and announcements are in both English and Cantonese. Tickets for single fares, ranging from HK$4–26 depending on distance, can be purchased from vending machines. Be sure to take your ticket when it pops up on the turnstile; you will need it to exit when you reach your destination. In 2008, the rail network linking Hong Kong with China through the New Territories was rebranded as part of the MTR network.

Ferries. The Star Ferry is not just a means of transportation, but a not-to-be missed visitor experience. The ferry crosses Victoria Harbour, connecting Tsim Sha Tsui with Hong Kong Island at Central. It runs daily 6.30am–11.30pm every six to twelve minutes, and costs HK$2.20; passengers aged 65 or above (upon production of HKID or senior citizen card) go free.

There are many other ferries connecting sections of the city: from Central to Hung Hom; from Wan Chai to Tsim Sha Tsui and Hung Hom; and the hoverferry service between Central and Tsim Sha Tsui East (near Hung Hom KCR Railway Station).

Ferries to the outlying islands are operated by New World First Ferry (for Lantau, Cheung Chau and Peng Chau, tel: 2131 8181) and Hong Kong and Kowloon Ferry (for Lamma, tel: 2815 6063). All depart from the Outlying Island Ferry Piers in front of the IFC buildings in Central. Fares vary, with the highest being HK$31. Jetfoils and catamarans to Macau leave from the Macau Ferry Terminal in Sheung Wan about every 15 minutes 7am–1am, and every hour 1am–7am; one-way fares start at HK$138, the cost goes up for the night service and at weekends.

Buses. The bus service in Hong Kong is good and relatively cheap. Double-decker buses run 24 hours (night bus numbers are prefixed by an 'N') and cover even remote parts of Hong Kong. Fares range from HK$1.20–45, depending on distance, and the exact fare must be put in the box next to the driver as you get on (note that all buses accept Octopus cards). There are three bus companies: New World First Bus (tel: 2136 8888), Kowloon Motor Bus (KMB, tel: 2745 4466) and Citybus (tel: 2873 0818). Major bus terminals are located on both sides of the Star Ferry, and on Hong Kong Island at Exchange Square.

'Public Light Buses' seat 16 passengers. You can hail them everywhere and get off almost anywhere along their route. Tell the driver when you want to get off and pay as you leave. Minibuses marked with a green stripe go to the Mid Levels, up to the Peak and to Aberdeen. You can find them in Central and along Nathan Road. Minibuses are red and yellow, and you generally pay when you get off. Maxicabs are distinctive green-and-yellow vans that run set routes and you pay as you get on (they also take Octopus cards). The fares for both range from HK$2–22.50. Destinations are marked by a sign in English and Chinese on the front, but the English is often smaller and hard to read. Both ply routes around Hong Kong Island, and in Kowloon, while a few carry passengers between the two.

Trams. Hong Kong's picturesque double-decker trams are also a tourist attraction and provide a pleasant way to see the sights. They traverse the north coast of Hong Kong Island between Kennedy Town and Shau Kei Wan. Pick one up on Des Voeux, Queensway, or Hennessy roads. Enter at the rear and exit at the front, dropping

HK$2 into the fare box as you leave. It's a flat rate regardless of the distance travelled. The service operates between 6am and 1am.

Trains. Hong Kong's rail link with China (formerly known as the Kowloon-Canton Railway, now part of the MTR system) runs 34km (21 miles) from Kowloon to the border. The local trains that serve commuters in the New Territories are an excellent way of visiting the area's towns and villages. Trains run daily every 3–10 minutes. Fares are very reasonable, costing HK$9 for standard class from Tsim Sha Tsui East to Sheung Shui and HK$18 for first class.

West Rail and the Light Rail Transit system (LRT) operate in the western New Territories linking the towns of Tuen Mun and Yuen Long. Trains run from 5.30am until 12.30am during the week and 6am–midnight on Sundays and public holidays.

Taxis. Hong Kong's metered taxis can be hailed on the street. Taxis on Hong Kong Island and Kowloon are red. Fares start at HK$15 for the first 2km (1.2 miles), and go up HK$1.40 for every 200m; there are extra charges for luggage (HK$5 per piece) and trips through tunnels (HK$20 for the Cross-Harbour Tunnel). Be warned that taxi drivers often don't speak English, so it's a good idea to have your destination and the name of your hotel written in Chinese. Many hotels print a list of well-known places in Chinese characters and English that you can carry with you to show to your driver.

Funicular. The Peak Tram funicular links Garden Road with Victoria Peak. The climb to the Peak Tower takes a breathtaking eight minutes; from the top there's a panoramic view. The tram costs HK$20 and runs daily 7am–midnight every 10 minutes or so.

R

RELIGION

Confucianism, Buddhism and Taoism or a mixture thereof are the major religions in Hong Kong. There are also Christian churches of every denomination, Islamic mosques, Hindu temples and Jewish and Baha'i houses of worship. Visitors will find Anglican/Episcopal services at St John's Cathedral in Central on Hong Kong Island, and at St Andrew's Church on Nathan Road in Kowloon. Catholic masses are held at Rosary Chapel on South Chatham Road in Kowloon. For information about services, see the Saturday issue of the *South China Morning Post*, which carries announcements from churches.

Kowloon Mosque (Jamia Masjid) catering to Hong Kong's sizable Muslim population is beside Kowloon Park, on Nathan Road.

T

TELEPHONE

Hong Kong's country code is 852; Macau's is 853. Hong Kong has 8-digit numbers and Macau recently made its 6-digit numbers into 8-digit numbers by adding the prefix 28 to them. The telephone system in Hong Kong is excellent for both local and international calls.

Subscribers in Hong Kong pay a flat fee, and are not charged for local calls, so if you want to make a local call, you can walk into any shop and ask to use the phone. Some shops keep their phone on the front counter. Public phones require a HK$1 coin or a phone card. Phone cards, available at 7-Eleven stores and Hong Kong Telephone's retail shops, have values of HK$25, HK$50 and HK$100. Hotels usually add a surcharge on both local and international calls.

For an English-speaking information service dial 1081; if you have difficulty in getting a number, dial 109. International direct-dial calls can be made from any public phone. IDD phone cards are available at convenience stores and at mobile phone shops in tourist districts in Causeway Bay and Tsim and Sha Tsui. You can use your mobile in Hong Kong providing it is GSM900, PCS1800 or CDMA. Operators sell temporary SIM cards with reasonable rates for local calls and SMS. IDD rates, however, are not very competitive, it's better to buy a calling card. Mobile operators include 3, People's and PCCW. For overseas calls dial 001 (10011 for collect/reverse charge calls).

TIME DIFFERENCES

Before you make any overseas telephone calls, have a look at the following chart, so you won't wake someone halfway round the world. The hours refer to the months when many countries in the northern hemisphere move their clocks one hour ahead (Daylight Savings Time). Hong Kong stays the same year-round, at GMT + 8.

New York	London	Hong Kong	Sydney	Auckland
7am	noon	7pm	9pm	11pm

TIPPING

Tipping in Hong Kong is somewhat confusing; tipping was never customary in China, although the British introduced it to Hong Kong. Who should be tipped and when is not always clear, especially inside China. Most hotels and restaurants routinely add a 10 percent service charge, but in upmarket establishments, an extra 5–10 percent may be expected; in inexpensive places, round up the bill or leave up to 5 percent.

Unlike in Europe, tourist guides do not indicate that they expect a tip; however, they should receive about 10 percent of the cost of the tour. A hotel porter should receive HK$5–10 per bag; an airport porter about HK$2. Hotel room attendants should get about 2 percent of the bill, but this is not obligatory. Lavatory attendants expect HK$2–5, depending on the establishment. Tip hairdressers/barbers 10–15 percent. Tipping taxi and limo drivers is optional; you can simply round up the fare.

The best rule is to tip according to how you feel about the situation; anything you give will be graciously received.

TOILETS

Toilets are not easy to find in Hong Kong. The best bets are shopping malls, hotels, and restaurants where you have eaten a meal or snack, or fast food places. Places frequented by tourists and up-market establishments will have Western toilets, both in Hong Kong, Guangzhou and on the islands. But you can encounter Chinese squat toilets in non-tourist areas or even in restaurants with a largely Chinese clientele; most of these in Hong Kong are clean and well-maintained. Toilet paper is not always provided, so it is wise to carry your own. To use a Chinese toilet, face the hood; be sure you put your used toilet paper in the wastebasket.

| Where are the toilets? | Chi saw haih been do a? |

TOURIST INFORMATION

The Hong Kong Tourism Board (HKTB) operates information and gift centres at key areas for visitors; the first one you'll encounter is the counter in the arrival hall at Chek Lap Kok, open daily 7am–11pm. The Hong Kong Island office is at Causeway Bay MTR station (near Exit F), open daily 8am–8pm. On the Kowloon side in Tsim Sha Tsui, an office is on the Star Ferry Concourse, open the same hours. The HKTB Visitor Hotline, tel: 2508 1234, operates daily 8am–6pm.

The HKTB publishes free brochures and literature about various aspects of Hong Kong; the *Official Hong Kong Guide* is a monthly information booklet with an overview of Hong Kong's attractions, shopping tips and current events and exhibitions. Free maps are available. Several weekly and monthly publications, free at restaurants and other outlets, tell you what's going on. *Hong Kong Diary* is a weekly publication; others are *BC* magazine and the *HK magazine*, both free from many bars, restaurants and bookshops. The *South China Morning Post* carries reviews and listings in its features section. The *South China Morning Post* has daily listings and an entertainment section on Thursdays. A new arrival on the scene is the fortnightly *Time Out Hong Kong*.

There is also a counter for the Macau Government Tourist Office (MGTO; tel: 2769 7970) at Chek Lap Kok, open daily 9am–10pm (closed for lunch and dinner). MGTO offices are at both ends of the Macau ferry terminal: Room 336, 3/F, on the departure floor in Hong Kong, and in the arrival hall at the Macau Ferry Terminal. Maps of Macau are available as well as the publication *Macau Travel Talk* and the pamphlet *Macau Walking Tours*.

Overseas you can contact HKTB branch offices. Australia: Hong Kong House, Level 4, 80 Druitt Street, Sydney, NSW 2000, tel: (02) 9283 3083. Canada: Hong Kong Trade Centre, 9 Temperance Street, Toronto, Ontario M5H 1Y6, tel: (416) 366 2389. UK: 6 Grafton Street. London WIX 3LB, tel: (020) 7533 7100. US: 115 E. 54th Street, New York, NY 10022, tel: (212) 421 3382; 10940 Wilshire Boulevard, Suite 2050, Los Angeles CA 90024, tel: (310) 208 4582.

TRAVELLERS WITH DISABILITIES

Hong Kong is not an easy place for travellers with disabilities. Hong Kong's frequent steps and its many steep streets, narrow crowded footpaths and the pedestrian overpasses on Hong Kong Island are not easily negotiated. However, some hotels have special facilities for the disabled, most buildings have lifts, escalators are common, and taxis are inexpensive and easy to find. Contact HKTB for information on accommodation and advice on services catering to visitors with special needs. The Society for Advancement of Travel for the Handicapped (SATH) has a website <www.sath.org>.

W

WEBSITES

HKTB's website is <www.discoverhongkong.com>. The *South China Morning Post* has a site, <www.scmp.com.hk>. The website for the Hong Kong Arts Festival, which takes place in February, is <www.artsfestival.org>. Macau's tourist information website is <www.

macautourism.gov.mo>. An excellent site for finding the best deal on air fares and booking flights and hotel accommodation is <www.travelocity.com>. For airfares try <www.bestfares.com>. All hotels offer internet access and many coffee shops offer free use to patrons. Pacific Coffee Company is on 1/F, International Finance Centre, 1 Harbour View Street (tel: 2868 5100); i-Cable Station, 2/F is in Ocean Terminal, Harbour City, Tsim Sha Tsui.

WEIGHTS AND MEASURES

The international metric system is in official use. However, Chinese measurements are still commonly used.

Food products are generally sold by the *catty* (1.3lbs/600g). Other items are measured by the *tael* (1.3oz/38g), and the *chin* (1.10lb/300g). For length, the *tsün* (1.5in/37mm) and *check* (1.2ft/37cm) are used in markets.

Y

YOUTH HOSTELS

Hong Kong's youth hostels are located in remote scenic areas, but are easily accessible by public transport. The main hostels are Jockey Club Mount Davis Youth Hostel, top of Mt Davis Path, Mt. Davis, Western District (tel: 2817 5715); and Bradbury Lodge, 66 Ting Kok Road, Tai Mei Tuk Tai Po, New Territories (tel: 2662 5123). For information, contact the Youth Hostels Association, tel: 2788 1638.

More centrally located budget establishments with simple or bunk-bed rooms include the BP International House, 8 Austin Road, Tsim Sha Tsui (tel: 2376 1111); Booth Lodge, run by the Salvation Army, 11 Wing Sing Lane, Yau Ma Tei (tel: 2771 9266; <http://boothlodge.salvation.org.hk>); and the YWCA's Garden View International House, overlooking the botanical gardens at 1 Mac-Donnell Road, Central (tel: 2877 3737; <http://hotel.ywca.org.hk>).

Recommended Hotels

Hong Kong has some of the most luxurious hotels in the world, with representatives from all the major international chains. Hotels listed below have full air-conditioning, offer 24-hour or limited room service, and a wide range of facilities. Hong Kong hotels have excellent business services and conference facilities; many have shopping malls.

Reservations are strongly recommended, particularly in summer and at Christmas. If you do arrive without making advance arrangements, the Hong Kong Hotel Association counter at the International Airport will be happy to arrange accommodation for you on your arrival.

As a basic guide, the symbols below have been used to indicate high-season rates in Hong Kong dollars, based on double occupancy, with bath or shower. A 10 percent service charge and 3 percent government tax will be added to the bill. In Macau, there's a 10 percent service charge and a 5 percent government tax.

$$$$	above HK$2,500
$$$	HK$1,600–HK$2,500
$$	HK$950–HK$1,600
$	below HK$950

CENTRAL

Conrad Hong Kong $$$$ *Pacific Place, 88 Queensway, tel: 2521 3838, fax: 2521 3888, <www.conrad.com.hk>.* A modern hotel set above Pacific Place with good views over the city. Rooms have classic furnishings with wood panelling and polished granite. Nicolini's is a fine Italian restaurant; there are also Cantonese, French and international restaurants. Business centre and conference facilities, health centre, outdoor swimming pool. 513 rooms.

Four Seasons $$$$ *8 Finance Road, Central, tel: 3196 8888, fax: 3196 8899, <www.fourseasons.com/hongkong>.* This five-star hotel has rooms featuring wall-to-wall windows giving spectacular harbour views, decorated in contemporary style with wood and silk wall panelling. Facilities to include roof-top pool, spa, gym, business services and fine restaurants. The hotel has an indoor link to the Airport Express station building and the IFC Mall, stocked with upmarket shopping, a great cinema and restaurants. 399 rooms and suites.

Island Shangri-La, Hong Kong $$$$ *Pacific Place, Supreme Court Road, tel: 2877 3838, fax: 2521 8742, <www.shangri-la.com>.* The outstanding feature here is a 17-storey atrium with abundant greenery. Large rooms with oversize bathrooms have dataports and views of the harbour or Victoria Peak. Continental, Cantonese and Japanese restaurants. Conference facilities and business centre, outdoor swimming pool and a 24-hour gym. 565 rooms.

The Landmark Mandarin Oriental $$$$ *15 Queen's Road Central, tel: 2132 0188, fax: 2132 0199, <www.mandarinoriental.com>.* Mandarin Oriental opened this boutique hotel in the heart of the Central Business District in 2005. The 113 rooms are large by Hong Kong standards and design throughout is warm and contemporary. Facilities include a bar, called MO, on the ground floor, the stunning Amber restaurant and a vast spa spread over two floors.

CAUSEWAY BAY/WAN CHAI

Empire Hotel $$ *33 Hennessy Road, Wan Chai, tel: 2866 9111, fax: 2866 2575, <www.asiastandard.com/hotel>.* A good value hotel in the heart of Wan Chai, it has many of the services and facilities of higher-priced hotels. Rooms are comfortable and pleasant with many amenities. Business and conference centre, health centre, swimming pool. 360 rooms.

The Excelsior $$$ *281 Gloucester Road, Causeway Bay, tel: 2894 8888, fax: 2895 6459, <www.mandarin-oriental.com>.* This hotel is located near Victoria Park, and hosts many tour groups. Guest rooms are spacious, and have views over the bay or park. Cantonese and European restaurants and an English-style pub with live entertainment. Business centre, rooftop tennis courts, fitness room and Jacuzzi. 884 rooms and suites.

Grand Hyatt Hong Kong $$$$ *1 Harbour Road, Wan Chai, tel: 2588 1234, fax: 2802 0677, <www.hongkong.grand.hyatt.com>*. A futuristic design of marble and glass, magnificent views over the harbour, and an art-deco style interior characterise this fine hotel. Rooms are smart and contemporary with luxurious amenities. There are three restaurants, including Milanese and Cantonese cuisine, a business centre, reference library, private boardroom, outdoor swimming pool, gym, tennis courts, golf driving range, jogging track. 556 rooms.

Novotel Century Hong Kong $$ *238 Jaffe Road, tel: 2598 8888, fax: 2598 8866, <www.accorhotels.com>*. This 23-storey hotel is a short walk via covered walkway to the Convention and Exhibition Centre. Rooms are small. Business centre, conference rooms, outdoor swimming pool, health centre, putting green and an Italian restaurant. 512 rooms.

Park Lane $$$ *310 Gloucester Road, Causeway Bay, tel: 2293 8888, fax: 2576 7853, <www.parklane.com.hk>*. Across from Victoria Park, this attractive hotel with modern marble décor is near to restaurants, shops and department stores. The top floor restaurant serves international cuisine with an Asian influence, and Stix is a bar/American restaurant/nightclub. Conference facilities and business centre, health centre, beauty salon. 803 rooms.

Renaissance Harbour View $$$ *1 Harbour Road, Wan Chai, tel: 2802 8888, fax: 2802 8833, <www.renaissancehotels.com>*. This spectacular hotel adjoins the Convention and Exhibition Centre on the Wan Chai waterfront. About half of the rooms have harbour views. Cantonese, Continental and international restaurants. Business centre and conference facilities, fitness centre, beauty salon, rooftop tennis court, jogging track, garden, large outdoor swimming pool and nightclub. 862 rooms and suites.

Wharney Hotel $$ *61–73 Lockhart Road, Wan Chai, tel: 2861 1000, fax: 2865 6023, <www.wharney.com>*. This pleasant hotel offers small but comfortable rooms. Cantonese restaurant, Western/Asian buffet, friendly basement bar. Business centre, outdoor swimming pool and whirlpool, fitness centre. 358 rooms.

Holiday Inn Golden Mile $$$ *50 Nathan Road, Tsim Sha Tsui, tel: 2369 3111, fax: 2369 8016, <www.goldenmile.com>.* This hotel is conveniently located in the midst of Nathan Road's 'Golden Mile' shopping. Rooms are a good size and modern with floor-to-ceiling windows, although views are blocked by nearby buildings. Fine restaurants including German and Cantonese cuisine. Business centre, rooftop swimming pool, health centre and sauna. 585 rooms.

InterContinental Grand Stanford Hotel $$$ *70 Mody Road, Tsim Sha Tsui East, tel: 2721 5161, fax: 2732 2233, <www.hongkong.inter continental.com>.* On the waterfront, with views over the harbour, this hotel near the Coliseum has hosted the likes of David Bowie and Elton John. About half the rooms have harbour views. French, Italian and Cantonese restaurants. Business centre, heated outdoor pool and gym. 579 rooms.

Kowloon Hotel $$$ *19–21 Nathan Road, Tsim Sha Tsui, tel: 2929 2888, fax: 2739 9811, <www.thekowloonhotel.com>.* A high-tech glass-and-steel hotel just behind the Peninsula, ideally suited to business travellers. Rooms are small but cosy, and equipped with with free internet access. Cantonese and Italian restaurants, and Western/Asian buffet. Business centre, beauty salon and tour desk. 736 rooms.

Kowloon Shangri-La $$$ *64 Mody Road, Tsim Sha Tsui East, tel: 2721 2111, fax: 2723 8686, <www.shangri-la.com>.* Relaxed atmosphere and good service in this newly renovated hotel. Rooms are large and luxurious; some have harbour views. Napa, on the 21st floor, offers Californian cuisine and a great view; there is also French, Cantonese and Japanese cuisine, business centre, indoor swimming pool, health spa and beauty salon. 700 rooms and suites.

Langham Place $$$$ *555 Shanghai Street, Mong Kok, tel: 3552 3388, fax: 3552 3322, <http://hongkong.langhamplacehotels.com>.* A modern five-star hotel in the heart of crowded Mong Kok, Langham Place prides itself on its use of technology, and shows a softer side with great artwork throughout the building. Rooms have floor-to-ceiling windows and contemporary furnishings. Stylish touches include a heated roof-top pool, Chinese-themed Chuan spa and free Wi-Fi in a laidback business centre that merges into its lounge bar. 666 rooms.

Majestic Hotel $$ *348 Nathan Road, Yau Ma Tei, tel: 2781 1333, fax: 2781 1773, <www.majestichotel.com.hk>.* Located in a complex on upper Nathan Road, this hotel offers plain but comfortable, contemporary rooms. There is only a coffee shop, but the complex has shops, a cinema and lots of restaurants. 380 rooms.

Marco Polo Gateway $$$ *Harbour City, 3 Canton Road, Tsim Sha Tsui, tel: 2113 0888, fax: 2113 0022, <www.marcopolohotels.com>.* One of a trio of Marco Polo hotels, it's located in the Harbour City shopping complex, a step from the Star Ferry terminal; others are the higher-priced Hong Kong Hotel and the Prince. It's a good choice for business travellers, with large desks in all of its good-size rooms. One French restaurant, but Harbour City restaurants are nearby. Business centre and conference facilities. 431 rooms.

Miramar Hotel $$ *118–130 Nathan Road, Tsim Sha Tsui, tel: 2368 1111, fax: 2369 1788, <www.miramarhk.com>.* This relaxed and friendly hotel has a great location overloooking Kowloon Park with a five-minute walk from the bars and restaurants of Tsim Sha Tsui. Chinese and fusion food and a slightly tacky nightclub. Fitness centre, indoor swimming pool and sauna. 525 rooms.

Nathan Hotel $ *378 Nathan Road, Yau Ma Tei, tel: 2388 5141, fax: 2770 4262, <www.nathanhotel.com>.* Recently renovated, this quiet and pleasant hotel near the Temple Street Night Market has spacious, nicely decorated no-frills rooms. The Penthouse restaurant serves Cantonese and Western food. Business centre. 185 rooms.

Park Hotel $$ *61–65 Chatham Road South, Tsim Sha Tsui, tel: 2731 2100, fax: 2739 7259, <www.parkhotel.com.hk>.* This is one of the best hotels in the moderate category, located across from the Science Museum. The lobby is attractive, and rooms are large and well-furnished. Western and Cantonese restaurants plus coffee and cake shop. Conference rooms and business services. 430 rooms.

Peninsula $$$$ *Salisbury Road, Tsim Sha Tsui, tel: 2920 2888, fax: 2722 4170, <http://hongkong.peninsula.com>.* Hong Kong's most historic hotel, first opened in 1928, is a study in colonial elegance. The famous English-style afternoon tea in the lobby is a must for visitors. Guest rooms in the newer 32-storey tower offer spectacular views; furnishings and amenities are sumptuous, and service is of the highest standard. Gaddi's is Hong Kong's premier French restaurant; other fine choices offer Pacific Rim, continental, Swiss, Japanese and Cantonese cuisine. Top business and fitness facilities. 300 rooms.

InterContinental Hong Kong $$$$ *18 Salisbury Road, Kowloon, tel: 2721 1211, fax: 2739 4546, <www.hongkong-ic.intercontinental. com>.* One of Hong Kong's top hotels, set on the waterfront, with luxurious granite and marble décor and harbour views. Guest rooms have spacious Italian marble bathrooms. Service is excellent and the hotel has some of Hong Kong's best restaurants. Business centre, outdoor swimming pool. 606 rooms.

Royal Garden $$$–$$$$ *69 Mody Road, Tsim Sha Tsui East, tel: 2721 5215, fax: 2369 9976, <www.rghk.com.hk>.* This is one of Hong Kong's most attractive hotels. All rooms open onto terraces overlooking a plant-filled 15-storey atrium with pools and waterfalls. Rooms are cosy and inviting; the most expensive have harbour views. Italian, Cantonese and Japanese restaurants and a restaurant in the atrium. Business centre, rooftop swimming pool and Jacuzzi, sports centre, beauty salon, fitness room, putting green. 422 rooms.

Royal Pacific Hotel and Towers $$–$$$ *33 Canton Road, Tsim Sha Tsui, tel: 2736 1188, fax: 2736 1212, <www.royalpacific.com. hk>.* This is actually two hotels, located across from Kowloon Park and surrounded by greenery. The Royal Pacific is the more moderately priced. Its rooms are attractive but rather small. The Towers is more upmarket, with harbour views from the highest rooms. The hotels share facilities. 673 rooms.

Salisbury YMCA $ *41 Salisbury Road, Tsim Sha Tsui, tel: 2268 7000, fax: 2739 9315, <www.ymcahk.org.hk>.* Reserve well in advance for this hotel, located next door to the Peninsula. It's one of the best bargains in Hong Kong, offering the facilities and service of much more expensive hotels at a fraction of the cost. Rooms are simple in décor, but comfortable and well-equipped. Restaurant and food outlets. Two swimming pools, fitness gym and sports centre with squash courts and climbing wall. 363 rooms and suites, 7 dorms.

Shamrock $ *223 Nathan Road, Yau Ma Tei, Kowloon, tel: 2735 2271, fax: 2736 7354, <www.shamrockhotel.com.hk>.* In a rather plain modern building, the hotel has a lobby decorated with chandeliers and artwork. Guest rooms are small but clean (cheaper rooms are without windows). 158 rooms.

Sheraton Hong Kong Hotel and Towers $$$$ *20 Nathan Road, Tsim Sha Tsui, tel: 2369 1111, fax: 2739 8707, <www.sheraton.com/hongkong>.* Located near the harbourfront, across from the Space Museum and Art Museum. Contemporary décor with Asian motifs. Guest rooms facing the harbour have great views. Restaurants include Japanese, an oyster bar and steak house. Business centre and conference facilities, rooftop pool and Jacuzzi, sauna and gym. 782 rooms.

NEW TERRITORIES

Silvermine Beach Hotel $–$$ *Silvermine Bay, Mui Wo, Lantau, tel: 2984 8295, fax: 2984 1907, <www.resort.com.hk>.* A pleasant if basic hotel overlooking Silvermine Bay on Lantau Island, a half-hour ferry ride from Central, and convenient for buses to fine beaches, country walks and the Big Buddha. Some of the rooms have been spruced up, also coffee shop and Chinese restaurant. The beach here is a bit polluted, but the hotel has an outdoor swimming pool, gym, sauna and tennis courts. 128 rooms.

Royal Park $$ *8 Pak Hok Ting Street, Sha Tin, tel: 2601 2111, fax: 2601 3666, <www.royalpark.com.hk>.* This hotel near Sha Tin's New Town Plaza shopping complex is easily accessed from the city by KCR or the hotel's shuttle bus to Tsim Sha Tsui. Chiu Chow and Japanese restaurants, coffee shop, squash, tennis and jogging facilities, swimming pool, health centre, business centre and conference facilities. Special facilities for guests with disabilities. 448 rooms.

MACAU

Crown Macau $$$ *Avenida de Kwong Tung, Taipa, tel: (853) 2886 8888, <www.crown-macau.com>.* One of the new breed of integrated casino resorts in the MSAR, Crown Macau opened in May 2007, raising the bar by promising 6-star service. Japanese, Chinese and modern-French restaurants, four cafés, a 6,000-sq-m (65,000-sq-ft) spa and extremely spacious rooms are part of its stand-out features. 216 rooms.

Posada de Sâo Tiago $$$ *Fortaleza de S. Tiago da Barrra, Av. da República, tel: (853) 2837 8111, fax: (853) 2855 2170, <www.saotiago.com.mo>.* This charming small inn is built around the ruins of a fort dating from 1629. Guests here are treated with true Portuguese hospitality. Rooms are in Portuguese style with furniture imported from Portugal and blue-glazed tiles; most have balconies. Macanese cusine at Os Gatos, classic Portuguese cuisine at Café Da Barra. Outdoor swimming pool. 24 rooms.

GUANGZHOU

Garden Hotel $$ *368 Huanshi Dong Lu, tel: (020) 8333 8989, fax: (020) 8335 0467, <www.gardenhotel-guangzhou.com>.* This hotel is well-named for its beautiful gardens. It is located in up-market northern Guangzhou, and has a spectacular lobby with a huge unsupported ceiling. Standard rooms have all amenities but a somewhat plain décor. Restaurants offer Western and Asian cuisine. Business services, swimming pool, tennis court, health club and dance club. 1,112 rooms.

White Swan $$$ *1 South Shamian Street, tel: (020) 8188 6968, fax: (020) 8186 1188, <www.whiteswanhotel.com>.* This luxury hotel is sited on historic Shamian Island beside the Pearl River. A spectacular décor includes a lobby with a cascading waterfall, and rooms are furnished with reproduction Chinese antiques. Cantonese, Beijing, Sichuan, Shanghai and Japanese cuisine. Business services, two swimming pools, health club, driving range, tennis courts, dance club and cruises on the Pearl River. 843 rooms.

Recommended Restaurants

Dining is one of the great Hong Kong experiences. The city is crammed with all kinds of restaurants, specialising in every imaginable kind of cuisine. Kowloon has a particularly high concentration of restaurants. It is impossible to choose more than a few from the vast range of possibilities. As everywhere else, the restaurant scene is in a constant state of flux, so it's wise to call and make a reservation before you leave your hotel.

The price symbols below are intended as a guide only, and are based on a standard three-course meal (or Asian equivalent), in Hong Kong dollars. These prices do not cover alcoholic drinks or such notoriously expensive items as bird's nest or shark's fin soup.

$$$$	above HK$600 per person
$$$	HK$300–HK$600 per person
$$	HK$150–HK$300 per person
$	below HK$150 per person

KOWLOON

Fat Angelo's $–$$ *Shop B, Basement, The Pinnacle, 8 Minden Avenue, Tsim Sha Tsui, tel: 2730 4788.* Open daily noon to midnight. A friendly uncomplicated American-Italian restaurant dishing up huge portions that can feed up to eight people. Children get an activity menu, but it also serves as a romantic setting with its checked tablecloths and wine served in tumblers. Other branches at 2/F Elizabeth House, Causeway Bay and 49A-C Elgin Street, SoHo, Central.

Felix $$$$ *The Peninsula, Salisbury Road, tel: 2920 2888, ext 3188.* Open daily from 6pm, with last food orders at 10.30pm. This restaurant is not to be missed: the marvellous view and the striking Philippe Starck design are nearly as important as the food. The Pacific Rim fusion cuisine is delectable.

Heaven on Earth $$ *G/F and 1/F, 1 Knutsford Terrace, Tsim Sha Tsui, tel: 2367 8428.* Open daily from 4pm until the early hours of the morning. This Chinese restaurant stands out as the most brightly coloured venue among the bars and restaurants of lively Knutsford Terrace. The menu crosses China from Sichuan to Beijing, with a few light modern touches.

Her Thai $$ *Shop 1, Promenade Level Tower 1, China Hong Kong City, 33 Canton Road, Tsim Sha Tsui, tel: 2735 8898.* Open daily noon to 11pm. Fabulous for its views of the harbour taking in the Central skyline. One of Hong Kong's most romantic settings with it gentle lighting and red hanging lanterns. Reasonably-priced and fine Thai food.

Jade Garden Restaurant $$ *Star House, 3 Salisbury Road, Tsim Sha Tsui, tel: 2730 6888.* Open Monday to Saturday 11am to 11pm and Sunday 10am to 11.30pm. Classic dishes, *dim sum* and seasonal specialities. Ask for the recommended dishes of the day.

Jimmy's Kitchen $$ *Kowloon Centre, 29 Ashley Road, Tsim Sha Tsui, tel: 2376 0327.* Open daily 11am to 11pm. One of Hong Kong's oldest restaurants, Jimmy's specialises in British food, but also has curries and other Asian dishes. There's also a Jimmy's in the South China Building, 1–3 Wyndham Street in Central.

Joyful Vegetarian $$ *530 Nathan Road, Yau Ma Tei, tel: 2780 2230.* Open 11am to 11pm. It is hard to find strictly vegetarian food in Hong Kong; most chefs add meat broth to vegetarian dishes. This restaurant is one of a handful that specialises in true vegetarian meals. From among the impressive variety of dishes try the delicious country-style hotpot.

Pizzeria $$ *2/F Kowloon Hotel, 19–21 Nathan Road, Tsim Sha Tsui, tel: 2734 3803.* Open daily noon to 3pm and 6 to 11pm. Despite its name, this restaurant specialises in pasta, with a menu that changes often. The atmosphere is relaxed, and there's a wide range of choices of northern Italian dishes. Pizza is also on the menu.

Spice Market $$ *3/F, Marco Polo Prince Hotel, 23 Canton Road, Tsim Sha Tsui, tel: 2113 6046.* Open daily 6am to 12.30am. This pleasant restaurant specialises in a wide variety of Asian foods: Japanese, Chinese, Thai, Indian curries, hotpots, satays and more.

Spring Deer $$ *1/F 42 Mody Road, Tsim Sha Tsui, tel: 2366 4012.* A Hong Kong institution, Spring Deer had been in the same location for over three decades. While the décor is tired, the friendly staff are not, and they rush about, serving up predominantly northern-Chinese food. The Peking Duck with pancakes and all the trimmings is unmissable.

Tai Woo Restaurant $ *14–16 Hillwood Road, Tsim Sha Tsui, tel: 2368 5420.* Open until 3am. Popular favourites at this restaurant include seafood dishes such as steamed garoupa or sautéed scallops. The set meals are a good way of sampling a range of Cantonese dishes.

Yan Toh Heen $$$$ *InterContinental Hotel, 18 Salisbury Road, Tsim Sha Tsui, tel: 2721 1211.* This elegant restaurant with opulent décor and great views over the harbour, serves exquisite and innovative Cantonese and Chinese food. The menu changes each lunar month.

CENTRAL

Beirut $$–$$$ *G/F–1/F, 27 D'Aguilar Street, Lan Kwai Fong, Central, tel: 2804 6611.* Open Monday to Thursday noon to 3pm, 6 to 11pm, Friday and Saturday, noon to 3pm, 6pm to midnight and Sunday 6 to 11pm. This restaurant offers an extensive menu of Lebanese specialities, including *shawarma* and *lahme bil agine* (a kind of Lebanese pizza). The homemade hummus is the best in Hong Kong. Ideal for lunch.

The Grand Stage $$ *2/F Western Market, 323 Des Voeux Road, Sheung Wan, tel: 2815 2311.* This good Cantonese restaurant is located in an attractive Western Market building that dates back to 1906. Great for dim sum or lunch after exploring historic Sheung Wan. After 2.30pm tables are pushed back and ballroom dancers take to the floor.

Habibi $$–$$ *112–114 Wellington Street, Central, tel: 2544 6198.* Open Monday to Thursday 11am to midnight and Friday and Saturday 11am to 2am, closed Sunday. Beautifully decorated with velvet seats, mirrors, niches with couches and hookah pipes. Great Egyptian food with a selection of hot and cold meze, including plenty of vegetarian choices. Weekend belly dancing.

Isola Bar and Grill $$$$, *Level Two, IFC Mall, Finance Street, Central, tel: 2383 8765.* Open daily noon–2.30pm, 3–5pm, 6.30–11.30pm. Modern Italian cuisine with a unique harbour view. This restaurant offers the chance to dine al-fresco on its outdoor terrace, or inside in its two-storey, all-white interior.

Jashan $ *1/F 23 Hollywood Road, Central, tel: 3105 5300.* Open Mon–Sat noon–3pm, 6–11pm. Extensive menu of Indian cuisine with dishes from both north and south. The richly decorated restaurant serves a good value lunch and a fine-dining evening meal.

Kiku Japanese Restaurant $$$ *1st Basement, Gloucester Tower, The Landmark, Des Voeux Road Central, tel: 2521 3344.* Open daily 11.30am to 3pm and 6pm to 10.30pm. A traditional pine-panelled restaurant serving *teppanyaki* and *sushi* delicacies, *kaiseki*, or *sukiyaki* or *shabu-shabu* set meals. The *à la carte* menu features Kyoto-style cuisine; grilled codfish and eel are particularly recommended.

Luk Yu Tea House $$$ *24–26 Stanley Street, tel: 2523 1970.* Open daily 7am to 11pm (*dim sum* until 6pm). This place has been around for 60 years, and is a living piece of colonial history with its carved wooden doors and panelling. It is a popular venue for excellent *dim sum*.

M at the Fringe $$$$ *2 Lower Albert Road, Central, tel: 2877 4000.* Open Monday to Saturday noon to 2.30pm and 7 to 10.30pm, Sunday 7 to 10pm. Consistently voted one of Hong Kong's top restaurants. The fare is experimental Continental with amazing desserts. Dress smart, take a lot of money, and enjoy the elegant and relaxing atmosphere.

THE PEAK

Café Deco $$–$$$ *1/F and 2/F Peak Galleria, 118 Peak Road, tel: 2849 5111.* Open 11.30am–midnight Monday to Thursday, 11.30am–1am Friday and Saturday, 9.30am–midnight on Sunday. At the top of Hong Kong Island for over ten years, Café Deco's open kitchen prepares international cuisine to please all tastes from steaks and seafood to made-to-share platters of Italian, Indian, Thai and Japanese favourites. Book ahead and be sure to request tables with the best views of Hong Kong.

Pearl on the Peak $$$$ *Level 1, The Peak Tower, 128 Peak Road, tel: 2849 5123.* Open daily noon–2.30pm and 6–11.30pm. Modern Australian international cuisine, based on the award-winning Pearl restaurant in Melbourne. Pearl on the Peak's top location, plus floor-to-ceiling glass walls, means you get spectacular views. The food is sensational too – leaning more towards south-east Asian and Mediterranean flavours.

WAN CHAI

American Restaurant $ *Golden Star Building G/F-2/F, 20 Lockhart Road, tel: 2527 1000.* Open daily 11am to 11pm. Popular Peking restaurant (despite the name), featuring northern Chinese dishes, such as seafood noodles and the classic Peking duck. Speciality is a 'Four Great Happiness', a combination dish of pork, beef, prawns and chicken.

Cinta J $$ *69 Jaffe Road, tel: 2529 6622 .* Open daily 11am to 5am. A friendly restaurant serving Indonesian favourites such as satay, prawn chili, fried squid and beef Rendang. Filipino dishes include crispy *pata* (pork leg) and mixed *adobo*. There are also Malaysian favourites. Live music nightly.

Fook Lam Moon $$$–$$$$ *35–45 Johnston Road, tel: 2866 0663.* Open daily 11.30am to 3pm and 6.30 to 10.30pm. One of the top Cantonese restaurants in the city. Seafood is the speciality. There is also a branch at 53–59 Kimberley Road in Tsim Sha Tsui.

Green $$ *Shop 7, The Sanlitun, 28 Harbour Road, tel: 2802 0666.* Trendy but easy-going Thai restaurant with plenty of room for outdoor dining on a podium above street level. The food is stylishly presented and offers good value. Popular with local office workers, Green's red curries are every bit as tasty as their green ones!

Viceroy $$–$$$ *2/F, Sun Hung Kai Centre, 30 Harbour Road, tel: 2827 7777.* Open daily noon to 3pm and 6 to 11pm. Indian restaurant with panoramic harbour views from an outdoor terrace, serving subtly flavoured tandoori, curry and vegetarian specialities, and an all-you-can-eat weekday buffet feast.

CAUSEWAY BAY

Cammino Restaurant $$ *1/F, The Excelsior, 281 Gloucester Road, Causeway Bay, tel: 2837 6780.* Open daily noon to 2.30pm and 6 to 11pm. Very popular Italian restaurant with an appetising menu of classic and modern dishes. Try the Spinosini pasta with lamb ragout and cherry tomatoes.

IRI968 $$ *28 Leighton Road, tel: 2577 9981.* This Indonesian restaurant first opened in 1968 – hence the name. It has since had a major face lift, and is now a funky joint, decorated in reds and browns, with a romantic ambience, a rarity in Hong Kong. It serves authentic Indonesian food, presented in a modern way, including *nasi goring, gado gado* and chicken curry.

Kung Tak Lam $ *Lok Sing Centre, 31 Yee Wo Street, tel: 2890 3127.* Open daily 11am to 11pm. This Shanghainese vegetarian restaurant uses only the freshest produce, mostly from its own organic farm in the New Territories. The vegetable soup and fried noodles are especially delectable.

Red Pepper $$$ *7 Lan Fong Road, tel: 2577 3811.* Open daily 11.30am to 11.15pm. The right place for those who like spicy food. Sichuan-style cuisine in a friendly, relaxed atmosphere. The staff will help you to order a meal that suits your taste; the eggplant with chili and garlic and the sizzling chili prawns are to die for.

Aberdeen Jumbo Floating Restaurant $$–$$$ *Aberdeen Harbour, tel: 2553 9111.* Open daily 10.30am to 11.30pm. Hong Kong's huge floating restaurant with its fantastic décor has long been a tourist attraction. Fare is seafood and other Cantonese dishes, not hugely overrated, but a popular tourist experience. The restaurant offers a free sampan ride to its craft through the typhoon shelter and back again.

Clube Militar de Macau $$$ *Av. da Praia Grande 795, tel: (853) 2871 4000.* Open daily noon to 3pm and 7 to 11pm. The atmospheric dining hall of the 1870 Clube Militar de Macau, with its high ceilings and arched windows is a rare glimpse into the past. The extensive menu offers excellent Portuguese cuisine.

Nga Tim Café $$ 8 *Rua Caetano, Coloane Village, Coloane, tel: (853) 2888 2086.* Located on the central village square, in front of the Chapel of St Francis Xavier, this alfresco café is a place to kick back, take in old Macau and enjoy Chinese and Macanese classics like African chicken and prawns in garlic.

O Porto Interior $$ *Rua do Almirante Sergio 259B, tel: (853) 2896 7770.* Open daily noon to 3pm and 6 to 11.30pm. Located on the Inner Harbour and not far from the Maritime Museum, this restaurant is notable for its colonnaded façade and its walls covered with *azulejos* and carved wooden grilles. The carefully prepared Macanese dishes are an excellent value.

Lian Xiang Lou $$ *67 Dishifu Lu, tel: (020) 8181 3388.* This outstanding restaurant is located on an interesting older shopping street that has survived in Guangzhou's relentless new construction. The décor is elaborate and elegant, and the Cantonese dishes are simply delicious.

INDEX

Berlitz pocket guide

Hong Kong

Eleventh Edition 2008
Reprinted 2008

Written by Alice Fellows
Updated by Ruth Williams
Series Editor: Tony Halliday

Photography credits
Axiom 36; Chris Coe/Jon Davison/Walter
Imber 20, 25, 41, 42, 46, 50, 53, 56, 58, 64, 78,
83, 84, 85, 86, 89, 90, 91, 95, 96, 97, 100; Dinah
Gardner 47, 61, 62, 65, 71, 72, 73, 75; Alex
Havret 9, 17, 18, 29, 35, 37, 39, 44, 52, 54, 55,
81; Hong Kong Tourism Board 27, 28, 30, 45,
76, 87; Richard Jones/Sinopix/Apa 57, 67, 68;
The Travel Library/Rex Features 22; Bill
Wassman 6, 10, 26, 31, 32, 38, 48, 98.

Cover picture: Mike McQueen/Corbis

Printed in Singapore by Insight Print
Services (Pte) Ltd, 38 Joo Koon Road,
Singapore 628990. Tel: (65) 6865-1600.
Fax: (65) 6861-6438

Berlitz Trademark Reg. U.S. Patent Office
and other countries. Marca Registrada

Every effort has been made to provide
accurate information in this publication,
but changes are inevitable. The publisher
cannot be responsible for any resulting
loss, inconvenience or injury.

Contact us

At Berlitz we strive to keep our guides as
accurate and up to date as possible, but if you
find anything that has changed, or if you have
any suggestions on ways to improve this guide,
then we would be delighted to hear from you.

Berlitz Publishing, PO Box 7910,
London SE1 1WE, England.
fax: (44) 20 7403 0290
email: berlitz@apaguide.co.uk
www.berlitzpublishing.com